Davy Jones

Words of Wisdom from A.A. to ZEN

Davy Jones

Words of Wisdom from A.A. to ZEN

M.H. Salter

<u>Other Books in this Series</u>

Peter Tork: Words of Wisdom from A.A. to ZEN

<u>Also by the Author</u>

Doorways
Dove
A Rose By Any Other Name
28 Day Novel Writing Challenge

For Dad,

Thank you for making a better world for me.

Love you more.

Foreword

To some degree or another, everyone is a paradox.

Even the most accomplished person has quirks and does things inconsistent with their best behavior. The philosopher Plato said the human personality is like a charioteer with two headstrong horses, each wanting to go different directions. The David Jones I got to know was like that charioteer, and his love for horses is part of the reason he landed in my home state of Pennsylvania.

Nestled between Appalachian greenery and misty hills, central Pennsylvania presents a patchwork of college towns, pastoral farms, faded cities, and quaint villages. Regional culture is informed by an Amish-Mennonite work ethic, with a promise that those who labor will find contentment, fresh air, and good fishing.

It was into this setting that Davy Jones of The Monkees bought a 14-acre farm in Beavertown, Snyder County. The property included a three story mansion, a spacious barn, outbuildings, and garden spots around the grounds. It was 1986 and he was flush with cash from a hugely successful Monkees reunion tour (in 1986-87, Monkees concerts were outdrawing The Rolling Stones and U2). Story has it that he'd stopped off there to visit a musician friend and bought the property in one sighting. Beavertown was an outback village (then pop. 875) with not even a traffic light, but it was only an hour from Harrisburg Airport. It became his seasonal getaway to breed, house, and train horses and chill out. In the English tradition of naming one's home, he called it Spruce Lawn.

Like countless others, I'd seen *The Monkees* TV show as a kid. On my tenth birthday Mom gave me the *More of The Monkees* LP. For Christmas, an aunt presented a pic sleeve 45 of "Daydream Believer." One of my first allowance-money purchases was a "Little Bit Me Little Bit You" 45. I was born in

Pennsylvania but had moved away in the 1970s. By 1977 my music career rooted me in California. My interest in The Monkees was rekindled while I was working in a used record store, an outpost for spotting trends. In those days, Monkees records were hard to come by (before CD reissues and streaming), so even beat-up copies of their Colgems records sold well. There was also a Monkees revival due to the *Head* film circulating on the "art movie" circuit (I love that film), The Sex Pistols covering "Steppin' Stone", and a New Wave gestalt that celebrated the garage band ethos of The Monkees, whose premise was of a start-up rock'n'roll band struggling to get gigs — which I related to.

One day in 1986, a Pennsylvania penpal mailed me a news clipping from The Snyder Country Times with the odd news that Davy Jones now lived near our old stomping grounds (we grew up about 45 minutes north of Beavertown). The Monkees were back on my radar, if for their remarkable comeback prompted by MTV broadcasting the original 1960's series. Some thought they were a new band, and their fanbase exploded all over again. Meanwhile, I pondered the irony of a big-time celebrity "Monkee" wanting to live in backwater Appalachia.

For personal reasons, I moved back to Pennsylvania in 1991. It had to be a call from God because, by human logic, Pennsylvania isn't exactly the locus of the music industry, but in 1992 I got hired as a house musician/producer at a well-appointed recording studio called Ascencion Multimedia/Susquehanna Sound. It was an impressive facility with roster of notable clients — including Davy Jones, living across the county line. I'd run into him playing pool at a local arcade, but he hadn't been to our studio for some time. I followed up, mailing him a studio-pitch letter and he was nudged by a mutual friend, multi-talented singer-songwriter Alan Green. Finally, in summer 1993, Davy rang me up and booked a meeting.

He arrived with his two English daughters, Annabel and Jessica, and after a lively bit of chat, he asked me, "Do you *understand* The Monkees?" He emphasized the word "understand."

I paused, looking across the conference table at this guy I used to see on magazines, and on the back of cereal boxes, when I wasn't listening to Monkees records that had sold millions. I can't recall verbatim, but my answer was, "The Monkees were the perfect fusion of comedy, music, and multi-media."

That must've been the right answer because he launched me on a long and creative journey.

Initially he hired me to help with sorting out his massive nest of old gear and media. Our first project was editing music videos, using footage from a 1992 concert at Six Flags NJ. From that came a VHS single: "Daydream Believer 1994" b/w a live "Girl" (the famed song from *The Brady Bunch* TV show). The late Jerry Renino was his bassist/music director, and his then-band included keyboardist Jim Riccitelli and guitarist Wayne Avers. When the band assembled it was a "guy's club" with constant laughs and pranks. They kept busy with concerts and on occasion I sat in with them as a guest artist. Davy dubbed me his "creative liaison" for getting things done with his audio-visual projects, curating through a mountain of material in diverse formats.

From that came the 4-CD box set *Just For The Record Volumes I-IV*, an archive of broadcasts, concerts, demos, interviews, outtakes, and rarities going back to his start as a child actor-singer. It documented his career around and outside of The Monkees from 1960 to the 1990s (it included clips from a "stoner session" with Peter Tork in 1968 and other Monkees spin-offs). Concurrently, we found the masters to his under-rated *Incredible* album (properly released on the 7A record label in 2024), and we began fresh tracks for his original songs, culminating in his *Just Me* series of albums, released between 2000 and 2004. All told, we worked on about 40 songs and took countless trips to studios in Pennsylvania and Nashville. At some point we were joined by Chris Andrews, a mega-talented singer-songwriter and actor who'd been a close friend with Davy since 1962, when they both performed in the hit musical *Oliver!*.

In that time frame I met Micky Dolenz and Peter Tork, and in 1996 I met Mike Nesmith in a Nashville studio, working on

Justus, the reunion album with all four Monkees. I sat on a couch and watched them juggle percussion instruments around like a scene from the TV show — or, to quote John Lennon, "Rock'n'roll Marx Brothers." As a songwriter, Mike had a few years' experience over Davy, who accelerated his songwriting as The Monkees took off. Their songs became album "deep cuts" because the producers deferred to ace hit-makers like Boyce & Hart, Neil Diamond, Carole King, etc. From my perspective as a songwriter and producer who respects the craft that went into these records, I rate Davy's "Dream World" (1968) as a chamber pop masterpiece, and he wrote other titles that I compare to early David Bowie.

Davy had worked in some of the world's premium studios, but for our recordings (made between 1994 and 2011) some sessions were impromptu and home-made at Spruce Lawn. We'd take breaks to critically listen to music, bingeing on ABBA, Hurricane Smith, Take That, Texas, T. Rex, and other favorites as he hunted for overseas hits that might break through in America. Then we'd go back to working on his songs. His remake of "You and I" (from the 1976 *Dolenz Jones Boyce & Hart* album) was partially recorded in his kitchen on an old tape deck.

It was during quieter times of kitchen table fellowship that I got to know a grounded, hospitable, and vulnerable side of David Thomas Jones. Every time I was over he laid out edibles and beverages, and there was almost always a stew on the stovetop. He loved to tell people, "I learned how to cook in grade school. I could've taken shop with the boys, but there were more girls in home economics, and you won't go hungry if you learn how to cook." Other times he'd have my family over to watch movies and meet guests from all over. He was a doting father and big on family. He outlasted the youthful trauma of losing his mother during his humble childhood in Manchester. He healed with horses and humor to become a globe-trotting equestrian and entertainer — The Manchester Cowboy.

One day he disclosed that he could be very hard and rageful on people closest to him (misquoting Chaucer, "Familiarity breeds contempt"), and I think everyone who worked with him was fired at one point or another, whether we deserved it or not. Yet, he was forgiving and exceedingly loyal, and he was quick to make amends with gifts and rehirings.

His boundless generosity was sometimes taken advantage of, and those abuses took a toll on him. For example, he was miracle worker at healing animals, even those on death's door. I recall this stray cat in terrible shape, and he'd invested time and vet bills in its recovery. He fell in love with that cat but, on some odd impulse, he gave it to a neighbor, later telling me, "I have no idea why I did that." That was the first time I saw him cry. A similar thing happened with a pidgeon that flew into his hotel room. It grieved him to let it go. I believe animals have souls we can connect with, and Davy modelled that connection.

In 2005, he brought me full-time into his touring band as a bassist-keyboardist and vocalist. At his insistence, everyone sang to give a full vocal sound. The set was well-trodden but we constantly had to be prepared to turn on a dime in case he'd make a sudden set list switcheroo (key change, obscure song) right as we were going on stage. Fans have provided us with many videos (my favorites are on my Youtube channel), and it's heartening to see we always delivered joy and a tight performance with Davy as the consummate showman. This band eventually became the 2011 road band for The Monkees reunion tour of Canada, the UK, and the USA. That tour was a critical and commercial success, sadly ending in "a glitch" as Peter described it. Davy went back to solo shows, experimenting in share-bills with David Cassidy.

On February 29th, 2012, I was sleeping on a couch in a California studio. My laptop pinged and I opened it to see an email from Bobbi Boyce, then acting as Davy's road manager. I was expecting to read details on an upcoming gig in Wisconsin. Instead, it was the notice that David Jones had died of a heart attack in Florida. My brain spun out, thinking it was a gag for a second before I settled on the brutal fact.

He was gone at age 66.

I went into some kind of shock and, in an hour, messages piled up on my devices. I spoke to a couple people then went on a sweaty hike up a nearby mountain. For months, I was overtaken with emotional outbursts and convulsive tears. It took me a year to finally stop feeling crippled by this loss, which happened while I was going through a divorce, the sudden deaths of my stepsister and a cousin (both much younger), and other traumatic downturns. I describe this hellish period as a "bottoming out."

I participated in a few memorials with Micky and Peter and former band members. Then my recovery from "bottoming out" began in 2013 when I met my future wife at a Peter Tork solo gig in San Francisco, and I wrote a song "Like a Big Brother" (to be recorded) that summed up my relationship with Davy.

Peter left us in 2019, and Nez left us in 2021, and I felt that like a tidal wave. Micky is still out there, flying the flag and powerfully hitting the notes. He celebrates his brotherhood with the creative souls known as The Monkees, bound together in timeless sounds and visions.

Of all the emotions I could feel about David, the first one is gratitude. He opened many doors and instructed me in stage craft, and as much as I could've wrestled with his irascible and shape-shifting but ultimately loveable personality, he was my true friend.

This "Words of Wisdom" is a compendium of his bromides and predictions — he prophesied the rise of Broadway Rock Musicals and spoken word recordings (dial up our collaboration "Exotic Animals & Beaches of Pennsylvania"). As for his wisdom and wisecracks, he was a classic comedian who could tell the same joke a hundred times (I watched fans mouth along with his monologues), but he always kept it fresh, telling me, "It's not what you're *saying*. It's how you *deliver* it." As I flipped through these exhaustively researched quotes, I realize that paradox creates wisdom of a kind. David once told me he was a bit sad he hadn't gotten a proper education, but he read often, and his street-smarts came from a full life of world travel and engagement with people from every walk of life.

I'm grateful he brought me along for the ride.

— Johnny J. Blair
2026

5·8·08

Hey John,

Thanks for coming to Wilkes-Barre with me I was glad of the company. — — —

Sorry your not coming to Epcot, plenty more on the books —

All the best

Davy Jones

18

Introduction

You can thank Peter Tork for this book.

I've been working on another project for a few years now — *For Pete's Sake: The Peter Tork Biography* (Working Title) — and during the time of researching for that book, my marriage broke down, I sought refuge in too much Pinot Gris, and I underwent a spiritual awakening, ego death, and complete re-evaluation of the meaning of life.

So while "being lifed", I kept hearing Peter's words of wisdom: *Be a hero unto yourself. Don't quit before the miracle. Get help, get help, get help.*

Although his advice had not been directed at me specifically, it still applied, it still helped me, it still put me back on my path.

That's when I *knew* that his advice needed to be a book unto itself. It could get Peter's words into the hands of others who might be wandering through life a little aimlessly. It could be a guiding light for others, the way it had been for me.

And so, once I was holding that book — *Peter Tork Words of Wisdom from A.A. to ZEN* — in my hands, I knew it needed to become a series that could therefore benefit as many people as possible.

And Davy Jones was the obvious next choice.

Davy wasn't just the "cute" one from The Monkees, he was a short man with a *huge* heart, and I feel this book is a vehicle to allow Davy Jones, even now, to continue to inspire and help others. He loved to encourage people not to give up on their dreams, to believe in what they do, and to always present the best version of themselves.

The quotes in these pages come from interviews and other sources ranging from 1966 right up until February 2011, just days before he passed away.

I have compartmentalized his words — mostly un-edited, un-filtered and un-salted — into relevant alphabetized topics. Need help with your outlook? Go to the section on gratitude. Had a crap day? Let Davy tell you some jokes that are so bad they're good. Want to know what Mike Nesmith was *really* like? Ask Davy Jones. Just need some daily motivation? Flip open to a random page and palm what little pearl is meant for you in that moment; use his words as your daily meditation.

Please know that whatever your situation, you don't need to do it alone.

Always be the best version of yourself.

Because no one can do what *you* do.

And if Oliver's Fagin can teach us anything, it's that you've *never* lost *everything*.

With love and understanding,

— Melanie Hyland Salter
2026

(I would also like to mention that Davy wrote two autobiographies: *They Made a Monkee Out of Me*, and *Daydream Believin'* [See the chapter on *Books* for more information]. *This* book does not contain any quotes from *those* books, and I would encourage you — if you are interested in his words of wisdom — to purchase both of those books written by the man himself.)

Hello Everyone.

Just a quick note to let you all know exactly whats happening in this groovy outasite, gear, fab, Super – or in my own words – Smashing Book.

I hope you will enjoy it and I think after reading it you will know the _real_ me.

Love to You

David Jones

24

Talk About Acting

I t doesn't matter if you're performing to one person, a hundred people, or a hundred thousand, I still give the same performance personally. I want to be as good as they want me to be.[1]

*

A cting is a job, but it's the sort of job you have to do super well because people are *always* watching you. You've got to remember that, even though you've sung a song, or done an act hundreds of times, the people who are watching you have *never* seen it before, so you can't let down your standards for anything.

You can't ever say to yourself, "Well, I'm not feeling so good so I'll take it a little easy tonight," because the audience will only have that *one* time to judge you on, and they get their whole opinion of you that one night.[2]

*

I f you want to be an actor you've got to be very much an individual. You can't ever follow the crowd in anything. Even if you just naturally want to do something, like everyone else is doing, it's got to be like you *leading* the rest, not you *following* them. You can't dress or act or speak like anyone else but *yourself*. You just have to be different if you're going to make it in acting. The four of us Monkees could pop out of a hole in the ground with bags over our heads and yet anyone would know which of us was which. That's what it takes to be an actor.[3]

*

You got to find something else. It's like, within a relationship between two people, you've got to have that *wall* there in between. It's formality, it's important that you treat people with respect; you've got to respect racehorses, you've got to respect show business, because anyone that's done anything — whether it be the bands of today: NSYNC, Britney Spears, Backstreet Boys, and all the rest of those people — it's not *easy* doing what they do and having a success and doing it, so I respect that. And anyone that starts talking down about this group, or that group, that kind of music; hey, it ain't easy, you know?[4]

*

An actor takes whatever is happening at the time, and then once they're tired of doing it and it doesn't feel good to them and they're not good doing it, then they leave. It's not everybody's choice. You hear from many, many people who say the same things I did. As you get typecast into a certain thing, people only see you as that. But my Fagin [in the musical *Oliver!*] was as good as any Fagin, as good as Alec Guinness, or as good as Ron Moody, or as good as Clive Revill, or any of these people. You just have to see that to believe what I'm saying.[5]

*

Y ou've got to respect the other people you're acting with, too. You can't go off and do your own little thing, especially on the stage, because everyone is a part of the whole thing and you can't ruin the balance. It's very important that, no matter who is up in front, the whole group shines. It can't shine if one person is always trying to hog the whole picture.[6]

*

I think that the most important thing for an actor is to be able to feel the part he's playing. If you can't feel it then it's just no good because you won't be able to make other people believe in you or in the part.[7]

*

I own a couple of racehorses right now, moderate horses, but if you place them in the right place, it's like, as I'm saying with the acting, it's where you decide to make your point, it's not in the training. Horses train themselves, really: you let them go for exercise in the morning, you feed them, you bed them down, and brush them over, they have a wonderful life. The secret to training racehorses is in the entering, it's where you *place* them, who you place them *with*, and the secret to that is, in my own head, keep yourself in the best company, and keep your horses in the worst. So that's the secret, and that's what I have in mind.[8]

*

I find as an actor, on stage, *stillness* is very eye-catching. You don't have to wave your arms around and be bigger-than-life to be seen or to be heard or to be enjoyed. I find that when I'm working with actors who tend to go too far, or to be broad, and to take too many steps, or whatever they might be, if I stand still… and I wait… maybe that extra beat… and *then* I deliver… then it comes back to *me*! If he takes it away somewhere, and he moves farther away — not on purpose or trying to upstage — it's something that I just do for me, it's a natural way of defending myself. I'm not a very selfish entertainer. I love talent. And it's no good being one entertainer that's good in a show — you've got 25 people in this show that are absolutely super. There's not a lot of difference between the top of the bill and the chorus line, it's just opportunity, it's chance. I don't say that I'm a great singer or a great dancer or a great actor, just that I've afforded maybe an opportunity more than somebody else has, so with that in mind I don't go into it sort of holding back, I like to go out and pump it out there, thinking, *Hey nobody does what I do*, so I'm not in competition with anyone.[9]

*

I like to get into the people's faces. I just realised after many years of being on the stage in the theatre, we have this third wall, and all of a sudden you find yourself, as an entertainer playing to the whole audience; I want to take in each one of those people, and I want to be able to have some kind of connection with each one through something that I do. I move around a lot on the stage; you know, I'm not a young guy anymore, but I like to dance. I mean you see Kenny Rogers, or Neil Diamond, it's like watching the Walking Dead! So I like to get out there and be in their faces.

Where did all this "spotlight" thing come from? You can't see the audience, you know? Forget about the third wall, let's get into this interaction.[10]

*

As an actor, I hope that I get the challenges to be able to go and do it, whether it be *The Music Man*, or some well-thought-of show, or part. I enjoy working, I enjoy being tested, and I wish that some people could see me sometimes, doing these kinds of things, because it's a total contradiction to the way people feel about you.[11]

*

They still make money from The Monkees, the company [NBC]. But it's not the fact that I'm *not* making the money [that upsets me], more the fact that it is taking up a spot. I'm glad *The Monkees* are shown, and I've been very lucky that it has been shown because over the last couple of years new fans have come in, and I've got a book out, and we've got albums out, and I'm touring, I'm very grateful for that — selfishly, I'm grateful for it. But on the other hand, that is taking air time where *new* product could be made. These companies that are putting out these shows — these old reruns, whether it be *Happy Days, The Monkees, Lucy, I Love Lucy, The Return of Lucy, Lucy From the Grave, Lucy Here She Comes Again*, or whatever they are — they keep showing all these reruns, they're not making any *new* product. There are actors out of work. When I joined Actors Equity in 1959 there were about 75,000 members; now there are millions of members. Actors need work, you know? There should be limited reruns, for a start. I'm sorry, but there should be. And at that particular point, we've got video machines, they've got these little cassettes that they can buy if they want to watch them, they show them in their own homes; they don't have to show them nationwide, you know? The TV companies are getting off cheap! We made $450 a week for doing *The Monkees* show. We got paid on the albums — I think we split five percent between us, so that would be one and a quarter pennies on every album sold. They sold 100 million records, so it's a lot of money, I realize that, but it's over twenty years since The Monkees happened. I was twenty years old when it started, so you can imagine, monies went here, there, and everywhere. I have absolutely no Monkee money left. The monies that I have now (and I own homes all over the world), the monies that I have left now, is monies that I've earned over the last twenty years, stuff that I've been doing in the meantime.

I have a TV show that aired February the 7th, called *My Two Dads*, I had another show I did, *Sledgehammer*, which I enjoyed doing, I have offers for theatre, which I'm very interested in. To me, that is it: the live performance. It's done, it's over with, I was paid, the audience paid, everybody was paid for doing it, it was a show that was done, and that was it.[12]

*

I used to love to watch *Happy Days* because they filmed with three cameras and it was a live audience, and I love live audiences, like talking to you now, I mean, I'm talking to you, we're having a discussion about The Monkees, about my career, about *They Made A Monkee Out of Me*, so I'm *on;* I'm trying to perform, and make it entertaining. I think [filming TV shows] has changed an awful lot for me because we were working with one and two cameras — stop, start, stop, start. Now they film stuff, you've got to learn your lines like you would in the theater, and if you don't do it right, then they re-shoot it, obviously, but *live*, in front of an audience. To me that situation comedy idea would be good, a very inviting project proposition for me.[13]

*

S ome of the movie stars that are there now — earning top bucks and are making five or six movies a year — they're all [short]. Sylvester Stallone is about five foot six [5'9"], Richard Gere, he's a little guy, he's only about five foot five [5'10"]. Not that *that* matters. I don't think talent should be identified with size or whatever it might be.[14]

*

I 've learned so much in the last three years, so in three years from now I know that I'm going to learn a lot more. I never took acting seriously, really. I said that it was fun, and never really had a part to play — the Artful Dodger in *Oliver!*, that was *me*, that was *me* at school, the only difference is, "I'm talking like this," instead of talking the way I'm talking now, a little Lancashire coming out, and a little American. I've never really had a *part*. In our last movie (in our *first* movie, we don't have a title yet), but I felt it was the first time I'd really had to *act*, that I really got a little feeling that, man, acting, that is something else! For the first time ever.

I've done a lot, I've done a lot of parts, I've done enough for being so young, I suppose, but I'd never known what acting was. What a feeling. I know what Lawrence Olivier or John Gilgan, I know how *they* feel now, I just had a little *taste* of it. Not all the way through the movie, but little, little tastes all the way. I was thinking: "God, acting, that's something else!" I felt much warmer, and I didn't feel as tight. I was doing all the comedy before, on the TV show, and doing all this kind of shtick, but I really got a little inkling, I felt as if maybe, one day, I can be an *actor*.[15]

*

As far as my career as an actor these days, I'm sort of limited to what I'm doing, only because of my own desire. *The Brady Bunch* was in the seventies. If I was acting, I want to be playing a *character*, I don't always want to be doing "Davy Jones". And unless you are fully dedicated to going out and doing that, making sure that you get that [part] and people see you in that light [as a character actor]. I've played Fagin in *Oliver!* since playing the Artful Dodger, and I'm "talking like this, my dear, come here, Oliver, lovely to see you, my boy," but they see "Davy Jones" as this [sings] "I could hide 'neath the wings…" and there's no getting away from that. There was, when I play the characters and I do the parts, but as they say, you've got to be working at it all the time. I'm involved as much as people want me to be, and I love the challenge that acting brings you.[16]

*

This time next year I might not be an actor anymore. I might change my mind. However, I will be an actor as long as I feel I can give a little enjoyment and make people laugh a little more. As soon as I stop laughing myself, I'll go into something else.[17]

*

Even though acting is a rough life, I love it. I realize that I'll never be able to do most of the things other people take for granted as long as I'm an actor but it's worth the sacrifice. It's the only job I know of where you can turn sadness into happiness right before your eyes.[18]

Talk About Addiction

As an entertainer, it's not the most engaging life in respect to your social times because you're so busy doing what you're doing to get the notoriety, that you spend a lot of time on your own. I think this is the downfall of a lot of entertainers who go to extremes — whether it be with alcohol, or whether it be with drugs, or just nervous problems.

It's all because you get this amazing *natural* high from performing, and all of a sudden it's not there at the end of the evening, or the end of the session in the studio, or whether you're on a movie set or whether you're on a stage. When you get off [stage], there's an amazing let-down, because you either go back to the room and flick the TV on, or you go to the bar and have a drink of your choice. But everything gets kind of old after a while, so you do tend to go back to the room, you close the door, and it's a very *solitary* kind of a life.

The winding down is very difficult. And then, if we're working two or three nights in a row, it's a late night and an early start, and you find yourself getting in a transport at 6'0 clock in the morning to catch a 7:45 plane.

It's very difficult to find that time, you've got to find time to be with your family, to be with your kids, to be with your sister, to be with your wife or husband — it's great to make appointments, and dates.[19]

*

For me, for everybody, it's the *down* times: this is the hardest thing for an entertainer.

This is why they, we, some of us in the entertainment world, they have bad reputations — they're into drugs, they drink too much, they beat their wives, they do this, that, the other. It's only because of the *pressure* of having to go to be a regular person.

Unless you can do that, you're not going to be successful in the long run. Most of our careers are like a little fish bowls, you go "*Bing!*" [up high] and all of a sudden you sort of go like [down low], and then it's sort of like that [up high again] and if you can keep it like that, highs and lows, and realize why it feels that way, then you're able to apply that to your other side of your life; it's very difficult. It's easier said in theory than it is in the act.[20]

*

Yeah in the sixties, we smoked a little bit of pot, and we did all these things, but thank goodness we didn't get into the things that destroy people's lives.

I can't say that I have a lot of respect for Janis Joplin, or Kurt Cobain, or Tim Buckley, or even Jimi Hendrix who was a dear friend, because I say (tongue-in-cheek flippantly), What would they be doing now? Shaking hands outside Caesar's Palace welcoming people? Or would they be able to sustain a career?

That's not the point. The point is you've got to *touch* people. And when you touch people in America you do it for *life*, because once you become a success in America people recognise that success and they revere it. So you've got to be very careful of how you treat yourself! And how you treat other people. You have to think from the end, because everything you do affects somebody else.[21]

*

I don't believe that smoking is hazardous to your health, I think it *must* do something to your lungs, but it's not the *cause* of cancer — that's a cop out because they haven't found a cure for cancer, so they've got to pick on something. Smoking is something that everybody does so I think it's a cop out because they've got no real proof that smoking does cause cancer. They haven't got it in black and white. It's an addiction, smoking, like anything.[22]

*

Let's talk about marijuana. In three years from now [1968] I think marijuana will be legal, and then all the people that say they don't [smoke it] will be saying they do.

You get addicted to something. Like, myself, I don't drink. I might go and have a beer with my dad or something when I go home, but when I look in the pub and see all these people that have been sitting there for twenty years in the same pub every night doing that, now *they're* addicted. They're addicted to beer. They go in, they drink, and the bellies get big. Now marijuana smokers are supposed to be "bad" and "evil" in this whole thing, but they're no worse than a beer drinker or a liquor drinker. At least people that are supposed to smoke marijuana, you don't see the [puffy] cheeks and you don't see the fat bellies. You know, I'd rather go and smoke marijuana than go and drink two pints of beer because I'd rather look… I'd rather be called a "junkie" than be called a "pot belly" because — a *pot* belly! How about that for a pun on words!

I don't think it's a *need.* I think, as soon as they legalize marijuana then there's not gonna be such a rush on it, you know what I mean? Everybody's doing it underneath the table, and having a quick toke, because it's all *illegal*. As soon as they legalize it… like anything. The reason they're *not* going to legalize it is because of the liquor laws: the liquor people aren't going to want people coming in, smoking pot, because they're going to go out of business! Nobody's going to be drinking this stuff that really decays your insides. At least they've proved that marijuana is *not* hazardous to your health.

I don't know why, but the laws, they contradict one another all the time. *This* is legal, yet *this* isn't. But *this* is worse than *this* is. So why not make *this* legal?[23]

*

I'm not Lindsay Lohan, or Robert Downey, Jr. I'm not out of rehab — yet! And if I *was* then it would be quietly done without the fanfare of some baby boys and some baby girls coming out the nightclubs at four in the morning, rat-faced. I can't say I *haven't* been! I can't say that I've *not* enjoyed doing that! Having a great time with the lads and playing some darts and having a couple of beers, and he would whisper in my ear, "How much is enough?"

All these entertainers I remember from the sixties and seventies and eighties, "You know who I used to be?" And they sit at the bar and people buy drinks, everybody thinks that they can go on forever, and that's the downfall of most people.

You just gotta know your limitations. If you don't know your limitations, then you gotta have someone next to you that *does*.

You know we tend to get very highfalutin and very above ourselves as an entertainer — we made all this crazy money and all of a sudden there is no more money. You live the means that other people expect you to. The benefits are great but the downfalls are even greater.

So, be careful what you do, lads, girls and boys out there.[24]

Talk About Advice

I'm not a philosopher, other than trying to direct myself in the right direction. So when I talk about this stuff it's only because I want to find answers for myself.[25]

*

I think, if I had any advice — or anything that I definitely can live by — it's that although you cannot set your sights *too* high in life, it is important that you do have certain goals. Have an objective you don't have to *struggle* to reach. And make sure, every waking hour of every waking day, that you're going towards succeeding in this particular thing. It's nice to set certain goals for yourself, and *standards*. It's something that I have done, and it's worked for me.[26]

*

You've got to let the curtain down. That's the advice I give. Find something else that you can do [in order to seperate from "work"]; I have horses, Peter has his beautiful house in [Connecticut]… When the curtain comes down, you're *this* person like everybody else. Don't exclude yourself.[27]

*

If I had a boy I'd help him out. Unfortunately I left home when I was very young and I didn't know anything about life. It took me two years to learn what my father could have taught me in two minutes.

You know how a father talked to a son. "Son, you're going out in the world…" That's a lot of baloney! They don't do that, but they *should* do that. I wasted two years finding out about women and life and everything I came into contact with. I had to experience all these things and I had a lot of bad scenes happen to me.[28]

*

You've got to keep your eye on each other, and be careful what you say. Words stick more than anything. Change the way you look at things and the things you look at will change. Always listen to other people's opinions and try to learn from them, and if you've got anything to add that's gonna teach them something then don't be afraid to speak up.[29]

*

Confidence and courage, that's what counts.

In life.

In show business.

Success is never final.

Failure is never fatal.

It's courage that counts.

That's why I have no fear, when I step out onto the boards.[30]

*

Grasp what you can — has always been my motto.[31]

*

Never give up on your dream. Never give up your dream; always try. You can't win if you don't get in the game.[32]

*

I said, "Give me a tip, dad."

He said, "Don't wash your woollies in hot water!"[33]

*

And as far as Fagin, the whole thing is just beautiful — it's an actor's dream to be able to just hide in that character and come out as… "this my dear. Oh, you're staring at the pocket handkerchiefs, my dear."

And at the very end, when he's lost everything, and he throws his coat and he goes to walk away…

You've *never* lost *everything*.[34]

*

W e can't give you grandeur or wealth, but from the bottom of our hearts, we wish you happiness, long life, and good health.

Thanks a lot everybody.

Listen to your hearts. Listen to your hearts.[35]

*

Talk About Aging

As a musician, I would love to entertain every day of the week, and perform, and give, and learn, and develop, because life is a very condensed place. And with the family and with the friends and with the time spent "working on" working, and all the rest of the stuff, it goes real fast.

I think we need to make some phone calls to the Powers That (Maybe) Be, that are not ours: Give us another twenty, twenty-five years, so we live until we're a hundred and twenty-five, or a hundred and fifty.

My dad used to say, "Son, son, it goes *fast*. It goes *real* fast."[36]

*

I suppose I've got to get older myself — everyone does, after all. But I don't worry about what the younger generation will come to, as they always say about anyone under twenty-five. And I don't think I'll ever feel old, either.

That reminds me of something my mother used to say. She'd say that you can always tell when you're getting older by looking at the policemen because they always seem to be getting younger.

It's very weird, especially in England, because the police look very old when you're young and then as you get older, they look younger. That's when you know that finally you're growing up![37]

*

Am I going to go bald? I hope not. I've only got one hair on my chest, and every time the wind blows, it cracks like a whip, actually.[38]

*

I don't touch [my hair] these days because it's going grey. But it doesn't matter; it might be an old grey cottage but there's still a fire burning in the grate.[39]

*

I'm a 54-year-old teen idol with breasts.

I go to the gym so they don't jiggle.[40]

*

I'm 54 years old, and I'm still a teen idol, huh? Well, I have tits now! All right. I'm a teen idol with tits, okay! How would you like to look at those when you go to brush your teeth every morning? I still only weigh 128 pounds, the rest of me is in good shape, I just got to find someone who wants to go halves with this liposuction job![41]

*

Time goes by too fast.

I'm sixty-five-years-old, and I don't get it.[42]

Talk About Books

I read a whole bunch of bits and pieces over the years, obviously from the fan magazines and the rest of the stuff, and I just wanted to give a little more insight into what's happening in my personal life [in *They Made A Monkee Out Of Me*]. I just wanted to put in my own two pence, as we say in England.[43]

*

I wanted [my autobiography] to be truthful, personal, something that people could identify with. I wanted to answer some of the questions that the people had gotten a bit wrong in The Monkees, and let them know that showbiz is not all a bed of roses.[44]

*

When I first thought about doing the book, *They Made a Monkee Out of Me*, I started to write first of all about when I left home, because that's when I thought my life began, when I left home. Then I started to take pictures out, and remember, and associate the times with pictures, and then I went through and found more pictures. And then I thought back to those days when we were all kids — my three sisters and myself — and we were all part of the Christmas nativity, or the summer pantomime, or a play, or whatever it was, and I got the pictures out for that. And then I thought, "Wait a minute, my life *didn't* begin at fourteen and a half." And I went back to the cricket, and playing football and running races, and even less than that, and I actually went back to times when I remember, when I look at these pictures, I couldn't believe that I was one and a half years old, and it was only six months prior to that that I took my first steps. And then I thought back on that, and then I remembered all these things, I mean even as far — as I said in the book — I have remembrances now of even feeding on my mother! And I've been trying to renew that feeling all the way through my adult life! (Not on my mother, though!) But, seriously folks. So, as it went along, I took the pictures out and I associated the pictures with the story.

Now I got all this together, and then I talked to a publisher, and he says, "Oh, we need eight or ten, twelve pictures for the middle of the book and they all go together."

I said, "That's not the kind of book I want to do."

"Well, it's not a fan magazine you're doing; it's not a fan book."

And I thought, I don't need to be talked down to, like this, by anybody. So I had to then think about it. The book [got shelved] for three years, not in its form that is now — it was not quite finished, there was a few stories that I still had, and as I went along over the next couple of years, as I thought of things, I wrote them down.

I didn't want to go the conventional way. I have all my life done things and handed them over to *other* people and they've given me a percentage of "me". And I didn't want this to happen with this book. And so I waited. Fortunately last year and the year before, The Monkees went out on the road and I was able to invest the sixty or seventy thousand dollars it took for me to put this book together. And it does. And if you're going to think about doing home publishing, you can do it a lot cheaper than that obviously, it's depending how you do it.

I'm very proud of the book. But once you've done it, just because you've accomplished that and you've spent that money, don't think that there's a *market* for you unless you load up your car go all the way to the supermarkets, to the different places, and sell

two and three and five books. I'm fortunate; I've made a
distribution deal with Dalton Books who have in turn sold to
different chains around the country, and maybe by the end of
1988 I'll be in a thousand, fifteen hundred stores, which gives me
— if I sold one book to each of those stores — that would be fine,
your sales are there, your expenses are taken out, but there's a lot
more to it. You've got to go out there and *promote* it, and you've
got to be doing stuff that's going to keep interest in "Davy Jones",
and this is what the book's about. That has already finished, that
is sort of like an ego trip, an autobiography, but then again, why
am I doing an autobiography at forty-two years old? I was about
thirty-six, thirty-seven when we first started it. Why? Well,
because thirty-seven years is a lot of life, and if I've got
something to write about, and there's an audience that wants to
read it. Well, why not? I hope to do more books.[45]

*

I've written three books, co-written a couple. *They Made a
Monkee Out of Me* was my first book, which I sold 100,000
copies of.

My second book was *The Mutant Monkees Meet the Masters of
the Multimedia Manipulation Machine*, which is mostly graphics
done by fans who contributed a number of pages for each.

And the latest book was called *Daydream Believin'*, which is
about to be reissued as soon as we get it off the press.[46]

*

The Book, *Daydream Believin'*, it's just a whole sharing memorabilia thing okay, obviously it's an update on my first book, *They Made a Monkee Out of Me.*[47]

*

I've written three books, I'm writing another book right now, it's called: *To All the Girls I've Loved Before.* It's not much of a kiss and tell, it's just some beautiful women and people that have been in my life that I want to put into a book form.[48]

*

I've written a couple of children's stories that I go to the local library in my little town and hopefully the kids are impressed by some of those little tales.[49]

*

There are writers sitting around with great stories and books that they've written, but until it's read by the *right people* it's not gonna be something that is on the bestseller list out of New York.[50]

*

They Made a Monkee Out of Me, Davy Jones, Dome Press, 1987

THE ONLY AUTHORIZED STORY OF THE MONKEES: THE 60'S PHENOMENON THAT BECAME AN 80'S PHENOMALY.*

"There are autobiographies… and there are ought-to-buy-ographies. This is definitely the best ography I personally can ever remember writing." -David Jones

"Fascinating… controversial… hilarious… yet subtly poignant, somehow. As the authoritative account of the entire Monkees phenomenon — it is unparallelled. As the story of my daddy's extraordinary life — I found it useful reading." -Jessica Jones (age 5)

"I haven't read it yet." -Peter Tork
"I don't want to talk about The Monkees." -Mike Nesmith
"Hey, isn't that errr…?" -Micky Dolenz

- CONTAINS OVER TWO MILLION PHOTOS! (he's lying-*Ed.*)

- DOZENS of them NEVER BEFORE PRINTED IN ENGLISH (that bit's true.)

Available in eBook, paperback, audiobook

*

Mutant Monkees Meet the Masters of the Multi-Media Manipulation Machine!, Davy Jones, Samuel French Trade, 1 June 1992

Original computer graphics by thirty-two macintosh artists with really warped minds.

Available in hardcover (out of print)

*

<u>*Daydream Believin'*, Davy Jones, Hercules Promotions, 1 January 2000</u>

From a Tony Award nominee, to the teen idol of The Monkees — Davy Jones: Daydream Believin' is a wonderfully revealing account of Davy's life and career. Davy shares his very personal recollections of his childhood in England; beginning with his time as an apprentice jockey, leading to his young days on the Broadway stage in New York and ultimately to his phenomenal success as teen idol of the 60's group The Monkees. Readers get an up-close look at his family life and career.

Let Davy make you a Daydream Believer all over again.

Available eBook, paperback, hardcover

*

<u>*Written In Our Hearts: Vegetarian Cookbook*, The Davy Jones Equine Memorial Foundation, 19 June 2014</u>

Born out of a simple idea for a simple fundraiser, the astonishing outpouring of response from the fans and friends and family of Davy Jones far surpassed all expectations and ultimately led to this book which you now hold in your hands. Filled with hearty, healthy, and delicious vegetarian recipes alongside fond remembrances, fabulous photos, and humorous anecdotes, this collection is the result of an enormous expression of love from around the globe.

Davy Jones was the handsome #1 teen idol of all time, but what many may be unaware of is that Davy was also a vegetarian and a dedicated horseman for the majority of his life. When Davy passed away unexpectedly, a great void was left not only for the people who knew and loved him, but also for his beloved herd of 15 horses, many of them rescued former racehorses, and all of them given the surname of "Jones." Davy's four daughters were suddenly faced with the daunting task of caring for these four-legged family members, and they quickly created the Davy Jones Equine Memorial Foundation so that their father's fans and friends could assist in fulfilling Davy's commitment to provide these horses with lifelong love and care. Your purchase of this book will merge with the efforts of individuals from around the world in helping to meet that commitment.

From recipes which were personal favorites of Davy's to the personal favorites of celebrities including Rose Marie, Florence Henderson, Jon Provost, Karen Valentine, Davy's fellow Monkees Micky Dolenz and Peter Tork, and many others — you will be delighted with a vast selection of tasty vegetarian and vegan dishes in many categories including not only such standards as main dishes and desserts, but also recipes for tea time and for children and pets as well.

Join us in celebrating the remarkable life of Davy Jones by enjoying this banquet of delightful foods and these fond, magical memories!

Available in paperback

*

<u>*When the World and I Were Young: Snapshots from the Collection of Davy Jones*</u>, Along Came Jones Media, 23 May 2018

In the summer of 1967, The Monkees hit the road for their first major concert tour. With the success of their hit TV show energizing fans, they were greeted with screams, hysteria, love, and applause everywhere they went. It was a lot for four young guys to take in. Fortunately, they all had cameras — Kodak Instamatic 104s, to be exact! From June through August, The Monkees were on the go-go. Beginning at the Hollywood Bowl, the tour took them from LA to London and everywhere in between.

Along the way, they introduced the US to one of their most ground-breaking opening acts: The Jimi Hendrix Experience! Whether you were there, or just wish you had been, this rare collection of candids brings the summer of 1967 back to life. Featuring many never-before-seen images of The Monkees, their friends, and even some of their fans, *When the World & I Were Young: Snapshots from the Collection of Davy Jones* is a treasure that captures the excitement and spirit of the Summer of Love as only The Monkees could have experienced it. Enjoy this groovy trip down memory lane with one of the hottest groups of the era, The Monkees!

Available in eBook, paperback

Talk About The Brady Bunch

I did a TV show in the early seventies, and I don't know if you remember, called *The Brady Bunch*. I did one bloody episode, okay. One episode. I took Marcia, Marcia, Marcia to the prom. Now for the next two years, I got hate letters from every other girl in America because I didn't go to their bloody prom, okay? I'm not kidding.[51]

*

When The Monkees finished in the early 70's, late 60's actually, we finished making the movie, *Head*, in '69, you know we all had our individual careers to start thinking about. I did a couple of TV shows — *The Tom Jones Variety Show*, and I did *The Tennessee Ernie Ford Thanksgiving Day Special* — but one of the most memorable occasions for me to go out as a solo artist was when I did an appearance on *The Brady Bunch* show, when I took "Marcia Marcia Marcia" to the prom.

Marcia was supposed to be the president of my fan club, and she said she'd get me for the school prom, or whatever it might be, because I'd written her a letter — and I do, I write letters all the time, I get lots of fan mail, and if it's not a personal thing that I write (I can't write everybody) then it's taken care of and people get whatever they're asking for: something signed, or if they've sent a picture, I do all that stuff, we do it. But *The Brady Bunch* is like, unbelievable, because people that didn't really see *The Monkees* — it's sort of like my daughter, some years back, saying, "Hey, Paul McCartney! Have you heard this: *Band On the Run*?" And she didn't know about The Beatles, but she knew about *Band On the Run*, Paul McCartney! So *The Brady Bunch* has been *something*. People think that my celebrity came from

The Brady Bunch, with my little blazer on — which I still have by the way; it doesn't fit so well, I can get it on, but it's kind of getting split underneath the arms every time I try it on for a joke.

I had a song called "Girl": "Girl, look what you've done to me. Me, and my whole world." Well, that was a song that I recorded as the theme song to a movie called *Star-spangled Girl*, which was a Sandy Duncan movie, and I just went on to advertise and promote the song. I thought it was a great idea, but, thinking about it, it was the first time that I'd ever done a TV show, which was like fantasy show, like *The Brady Bunch*, or *Friends*, or whatever it might be, where they actually used "Davy Jones", the celebrity. So that was a new plateau of relating for me as well, all of a sudden.

The Monkees just came as a normal thing for me; I'd been on Broadway, and that was just another gig. But after *The Brady Bunch* it was different because all of a sudden I said, "Well, yeah I guess I *am* a celebrity; I guess I *am* 'Davy Jones from *The Monkees*', and I'm on *The Brady Bunch*, which is another fantasy show."

And then the movie came along, and they asked me to be in the movie, and I said, "By all means, yeah!" It was great fun and they sort of spoofed it up a little bit, and they had middle-aged women there screaming, "Oh, Davy!" and the young kids going, "What are they doing this for?" But it happens all the time now, we go do concerts and little kids are there with their parents, baby boomers, and they're my age, and they bring their kids and so the kids are looking at the mom getting wobbly knees, saying hello to Davy Jones 35 years later. So it's all been an enriching experience you know. And it continues to be.[52]

*

Well, that song ["Girl"] was recorded for a Sandy Duncan movie called *Star Spangled Girl*, and I recorded that song especially for that, I was hired to sing the title song to a movie! It was never released as a single. It was never really put on a CD, an album, a record… but then everybody remembers that song and enjoyed it in *The Brady Bunch* TV show, *Brady Bunch Movie*.[53]

*

TV Land nominated me for Most Memorable Episode and I think I won the award. The next year they nominated me for something else; I couldn't make it because I was working and all three Catwomen were there, so if I'd known that I would have cancelled and got there, you know? Because I'm a little partial to a bit of… you know… Yvonne Craig actually played my wife in an episode of Ben Casey back in 1964, so when they start rerunning that you'll see that I was a wife-beating glue-sniffer! "Talkin like this mate, you know, it's alright."

I never thought about [whether the girls on *The Brady Bunch* were fans], I tried to be natural and I talked to them as if I was Davy Jones, this guy who was visiting. I knew the premise of the TV episode and I'd seen *The Brady Bunch*, I just couldn't understand why — if this guy was an architect — why they were living in two rooms! Hello? You should have built another room, mate.[54]

*

Miss Marcia Brady,
President, Davy Jones Fan Club
Dear Marcia:

I want to thank you for your interest in my career. Without the help of people like you, my career would not be possible.

If I'm ever in your city, I'll be happy to show my appreciation any way I can.

With best wishes, I am your friend, always

Davy Jones

Talk About Career

Getting an early start in a career is necessary today. The sooner you pick a career and start working on it, the higher up you'll be by the time you're thirty.[55]

*

She [my mother] saw me in the school play, and she saw me in the church Christmas Nativity, and I remember her saying to my father, "David wants to do this; he wants to be an actor. And if he wants to… he will. He will."[56]

*

There had always been music in my family. My mother was a pianist, my sisters sang and I just fell into amateur dramatics naturally.[57]

*

I'd gotten in some plays that the Congregational Church my family went to. I didn't get the big roles in these plays. Mostly a guy called John Jones got the really good parts. But I didn't mind because I wasn't really that interested in acting then.[58]

*

The only reason I started acting was because it was a good way to get out of classes at school. We used to have school plays and I'd tell my teachers that I had to learn my lines and they'd excuse me. I didn't actually want to act at that time, just wanted to get out of school.[59]

*

To make up for being "rejected" for the church choir, I would sing in hospitals. I would ring up and say, "I'm gonna come sing for your patients." And they would say, "Groovy."

I would go down and sing rock and roll songs to the sick people! My favorite singers then, believe it or not, were Linda Scott and Bobby Vee! I dreamed of someday getting to meet them.[60]

*

I would perform in the school plays, but I'd seldom get leading roles because I was too small. I did get one major part that I loved doing — I played Tom Sawyer. I had to learn 1,000 pages of dialogue, but I learn things very easily when I have to. Things that aren't forced on me take a lot longer. If someone said to me, "Know this script in an hour or I'll shoot you," I'd learn the whole thing easily.[61]

*

I got my first chance to act through answering a BBC advertisement for boys to play urchins. They asked me to audition but I didn't get a job. So I answered the same advertisement a second time. They obviously didn't remember me. I did the same audition and was accepted. [BBC Sunday-Night Play, Summer Theatre: June Evening, as Benny Whittle, 1960] So I started acting then, a couple of spots on radio, little plays like *Morning Story*. Everybody at school said I should be a professional actor, but I always said, "No." I was going to be a jockey.[62]

*

When I was a little kid I always wanted to be a jockey because I was shorter than most.[63]

*

My father used to take me to Manchester racecourse and suggested that when I left school, because I didn't have the height, the size or capacity to do a carpentry or plumbing apprenticeship, I should try racing. We actually contacted the Manchester Evening News who put us in touch with Basil [Foster] in Newmarket.[64]

*

I really decided that I wanted to be a jockey because I realised it was the one profession in which it was an advantage to be little. Luckily enough, one of my sisters knew a bloke who was friendly with a reporter called Richard Onslow on the

Sporting Chronicle. Onslow knew Basil Foster, the well-known Newmarket trainer, and wrote to him on my behalf.[65]

*

I spent six weeks with Basil after I'd left school earlier than I should have done, in December 1961, and went to work for him as an apprentice. I was galloping up Warren Hill after only a few weeks and loving every minute of it. Being a cocky kid, I even went into the stable lads boxing championship. I got a good walloping from Taffy Thomas — that was an awakening — and now I can honestly say that I'm all mouth and trousers![66]

*

I had watched the races on TV and always dreamed of being a jockey, so when I was 14 I left home and went to train to be a jockey. I hated school at the time, but after I left I really regretted it. I regretted it because it was a very hard life in the stables.[67]

*

It was terribly hard. I cried nearly every night. The masters would give you "horsebites" (pinch your legs until they got red) and they hurt awfully. They were really hard on us in order to make us "tough."[68]

*

When I left home… that's when I thought my life began, when I left home. Going to the stables… what the feeling was at fourteen and a half, fifteen, to leave home and go two-hundred miles away and live in a caravan and work with horses from four-thirty in the morning 'til six o'clock at night, and then go to sleep dog-tired, and wake up, and do it all again. And never having been away from home, never even worked with horses, and all of a sudden here I am, supposedly like a grown-up, you know what I'm saying? That was a very difficult period in my life. I remembered all the feelings, and all the anxieties I had when I first left home. You'll experience it. Everybody experiences it. It's a very traumatic thing. And either it's over fast, or it goes on for three months. I was very frightened, I didn't like being on my own, away from my family.[69]

*

When my mum passed away, my dad said, "Son, I never want to see you in overalls."

I said, "But Dad, you've been in overalls all your life!"

He says, "So that *you* don't have to wear them."[70]

*

It was hard for him. My dad loves me and I love him, but he wanted me to get out into the world and make it. He encouraged me to be a jockey and even sent money while I was training. Later, he encouraged me to be an actor. He just didn't want me to end up like him. He has to rely on me now, even if he doesn't like it. If he's broke, he wouldn't say a word.

He'd starve first. If I didn't send home a penny, he'd never ask why.[71]

*

I was training to be a jockey, but I realized that it would take a lot of time before I would be making any amount of money at all. It wasn't until I was out on my own and fed up with being broke that I got interested in acting as a real job.

I started doing small weekend acting jobs while I was still in jockey's training.[72]

*

I had been doing acting jobs on the weekends occasionally and the time came when I had to choose between the two occupations [acting or horse riding].[73]

*

After four or five months, a theatrical agent who knew Basil spent the day shooting with us. In the car on the way home, Basil mentioned that I was in show business. I had that confidence and had spent all day cracking jokes.

He insisted I went, and I just cried; I wanted to be a jockey.

But he said "You're going! Come back when you're famous."[74]

*

I'm saying, "No, no, I want to be a jockey."

The trainer [Basil Foster] said to me, "Be an actor. Make a lot of money. And come back and own horses."

So that's always been in my mind.[75]

*

I didn't want to leave the stables at all, even for a few weeks. Being a jockey was my big ambition, not acting. But Basil persuaded me to try it for a time, so I travelled up to London to audition for the part of Michael in a touring company production of *Peter Pan*. They had me walk about, say a few lines, sing a song, and eventually they said I was fine for the part.

They also sent me for an audition for the part of the Artful Dodger in Lionel Bart's West End production of *Oliver!*, but the person who auditioned me said I could only have the part if I lost my Northern accent. I had just six weeks to do it while I was touring with *Peter Pan*. It was all a bit of a laugh really, but Jane [Asher] did manage to teach me enough phrases to pass the second audition when I got back to London.[76]

*

When I was in the stables in 1961, the agents came — other actors owned horses, so that's why they were there — and they took me to London. I rehearsed the song: *"Consider yourself at home, Consider yourself one of the family..."*

"All right, and what's your name?"

"David Jones."

"And where do you come from?"

"I come from Manchester."

"Uh, excuse me, but... do you speak like all the time?" [with a heavy Manchester accent.]

"Yes, I do. You're right there, I do."

They gave me six weeks to go away and come back having learned a Cockney accent. Me trying to sing in a Cockney accent... it's like Mick Jagger trying to sing like he's from the South![77]

*

I was in England, I was 15 years old, and I was in a show called *Oliver!*. I played the Artful Dodger. And David Merrick, the big Broadway producer, came over to see the show before it opened on Broadway — because they had another company over in America — and for the first time he could understand what the Artful Dodger was saying! Being a Manchester boy, I had to learn how to "talk like that", so I was talking very slowly, and it was the first time he could understand what the Dodger had said. That was a Friday night. On Sunday morning, I was on a plane with David Merrick coming to America. I opened on Broadway two weeks later.[78]

*

David Merrick came over to see the production in England, and he came backstage to me and asked, "Would you like to come to America?"

I said, "Who are you? Maverick?" Because I didn't know who he was.

"No, *Merrick*. David Merrick. Would you like to go to America?"

"No, I'm not, I'm going back to the stables. I'm almost finished. I'm going back to be a jockey."

"Well, we want you to come over to America."

And the reason why he asked *me* was to replace the current boy that was doing it (Michael Goodman) and to give Georgia, and the rest of the cast, lessons in how to speak, because nobody could understand what anybody was saying! And me being from Manchester, I talked like this: "All right, Fagin, I'd like to say, it's nice to see ya, because I'm talking very slowly, 'cause I'm wanting to sound like I come from London."[79]

*

I had always wanted to go to Canada. I'd tell my girlfriends at school that I was going to Canada someday (not knowing I really would be, of course) and this would really impress them.[80]

*

I went to Toronto, spent a week there in a room at the Royal York Hotel, and finally they put me in the show. The stage was three times as long as this [indicating the table] and the stage that I'd come from was no bigger than this [indicating his coffee cup] and it was *amazing*.

But I was like an orphan. No one would speak to me, no one would accept me. Except for Georgia.[81]

*

When they told the boy who was playing the Dodger he'd have to leave, the cast was terribly upset. And without even knowing me, they turned against me.[82]

*

We went to New York. We opened without reviews in the newspapers, because they were on strike. David Merrick called up Walter Winchell, Clive Barnes, and a number of other reporters… except they *weren't* those people. They were just names in the phone book that were the same! But he said, "Walter Winchell says this is a smash! Clive Barnes says this is the best thing he's ever seen!" And he put them on the billboards outside… without, of course, saying that it was Walter Winchell from New Jersey, or Clive Barnes from Virginia, or wherever. Smart man.[83]

*

I was still very green and very nervous. Opening night was a pretty frightening event. After all, it was my first "opening" — *Oliver!* had been going for two and a half years when I joined.

My first lines came after the show had been going on for 35 minutes. I walked on stage, then, out of the corner of my eye, I saw a late couple walking down the aisle to take their places in the front row.

I turned and said, "Oh, I'm glad you could make it, we've been waiting for you," or something like that, and it broke the audience up. I'd just gone straight out of character and started talking to these people up front, and they threw back beautiful lines, which I could really handle. And then we went on with the show.[84]

*

It was fantastic. We opened the papers — and I'd gotten all the reviews! They hardly mentioned another person. They raved about me.

But it was funny, I still didn't feel like anything because until that moment, nobody wanted to know me.[85]

*

I didn't have too many friends [in New York], but I wasn't lonely because I was always getting invites to dinner. People would come and see the show and they'd come backstage and invite me out. I've forgotten much of that time, but I can remember one very funny incident.

My first cue every night was at five minutes after nine. We were always supposed to be at the theater by eight o'clock, but I would always go across the street to a little restaurant and have a soda.

Well, one night my watch wasn't set right and as I strolled in from my evening soda I heard my cue to come on stage! In 30 seconds I scrambled up three flights of stairs to my dressing room, threw on my cape and hat, pulled up my long pants (we wore knickers in the show) and ran on stage. I was really scared, but no one ever found out![86]

*

I think when the Dodger comes out onto the stage, and he sort of stalks around this little character who's lost in the middle of London, and I just took myself to that particular time. I was this undersized 18 year old — that's what it says in the script: an undersized 18 year old. Well, I was 15 when I started the part — but I had a certain sort of maturity about me because it was a confidence that I had, therefore it fitted the role. When the artful dodger stalked Oliver, and he stands there and he's sort of posing and he's being looked at — I know when I'm sort of getting eyes from somebody or whatever, and I play on it a little bit, you know, when I'm flirting with a girl or something like that. So I'm sort of flirting with this little guy, and he looks at me, and I know he's looking at me, and I'm sort of polishing my nails, and I go [double take], "What you staring at? Ain't you never seen a gent?" (You know, I'm doing this whole show for him.) From there on in, that established that character. I've seen other kids do it, I've seen other people do the thing, and unless that's right, right there, you can do it throughout the show and really re-establish yourself.

And the other favourite part was when they catch him at the very end, and he goes, "Who do you think you're laying your hands on? Assault and battery, that's what it is!" And he says, "I'll call my attorney, only he's having breakfast with the House of Commons!" So he's a cheeky little character.[87]

*

Georgia was nominated, Clive [Revill] was nominated, and I was nominated for Tony Awards.

And I remember going to the Tony Awards, and they said, "And the winner for Best Supporting Actor: David…"

And I leaned forward in my seat…

And they said somebody *else's* name.

But I'm glad it *wasn't* me that won, because that guy died six months later. It could've been me![88]

*

I've never been a terribly ambitious actor because I always thought my acting skills were just a natural thing when I was a kid. And with the Tony nomination, well I was lucky, you know. Anyway, if I had won it, I probably wouldn't have known what to say and I'd probably wouldn't have been able to be seen or reach the microphone at the time![89]

*

There was quite a few other people that got their start in that particular show [*Oliver!*], in that theatrical production: people like Phil Collins, he was in the show, and through the years I've noted a lot of other people that have gone on to entertain.[90]

*

In the audience [of *Oliver!*], not only was there Judy Garland, Frank [Sinatra] and Sammy Davis, and lots of other celebs, Buddy Rich who became a friend, and all these people came to see the show, but also some executives from Columbia Pictures.

And they saw me and soon after, came to see me at the theatre and offered me a contract. In 1963 I was signed to Columbia Pictures on a long-term picture deal. Then they had to find the right vehicle for me.

During certain periods of release [from *Oliver!*] — it was on for two and a half years on Broadway — they took me to Hollywood, and I was in Ben Casey, I was in The Farmer's Daughter, Bewitched, all those shows in the early sixties. I auditioned for Hogan's Heroes, I auditioned for Wackiest Ship in the Army, and none of it happened until '65 when The Monkees idea came along.[91]

*

I spent two years on Broadway, and seven months on the road with the *Oliver!* company. Then I got a call to do *Pickwick* in Hollywood. I did it for one reason: to show the people, who hadn't seen me, what I could do. I also did a *Ben Casey* show and *The Farmer's Daughter* show… I spent three months in England. I went home and rode again. I rode 17 winners, which shows I didn't forget what I learned![92]

*

To tell the truth, I wasn't sure what 1 was going to do [after *Oliver!*]. Things looked so bleak that I was ready to forget show business and just stay at home [in England]. Months passed and I heard nothing from my manager or agents in America, so I began thinking seriously about racing again. Then in March 1965 I received word from Ward Sylvester to return immediately to America. Once more I was faced with the decision of leaving England for something unknown. But I felt I had to go back, if only to make my father proud of me.[93]

*

I made one huge mistake. When The Monkees finished in 1969/70, I should have got away from Hollywood and got back into the racing game. Instead, I waited another 10 years. Everyone makes mistakes in life and for me that was the biggest.[94]

*

I did [feel bad about performing]. In the Eighties, I went back to England in '82 and I said to myself, "I'm not going to do [acting]."

Then all of a sudden, I'm watching television and seeing what's going on, and I said, "I'm better than *this*. I should be doing some work."

So in '86, I played the part of Jesus Christ in *Godspell*, and I went out there for a year and I just renewed my interest in the business. I hadn't worked [as a performer] for about four years in England, I was just looking after horses and taking care of stuff, and I thought, "I *can* do this. I've got to go there and do this."

And so I did. And then we did the '86 Monkees reunion tour, which was the biggest tour of the year. And basically I'm just trying to incorporate my enthusiasm into my performance.[95]

*

I enjoyed playing Jesus [in *Godspell.*] The only thought I had once in a while as I was singing, "Oh God, I'm Dying", was that someone from the audience would shout out "Could you give us 'Daydream Believer' before you go?"[96]

*

Last year [1993] I toured in *Oliver!* once again. My kids said it was time I acted my age! So I was Fagin. It's a great part. It's a great show. And I'm a great supporter of theatre, I love theatre. And to play Fagin was a great plan for me, because it took me into people's hearts as a different sort of a character, not this little guy that got the girls. I'm talking like this [puts on character voice], "Come 'ere, sit down by the fire. Dodger!" And I got the makeup, and I felt like Fagin, and I felt that *my* Fagin was as good as a few that I've seen, and I wasn't afraid of it. You *can't* be afraid.[97]

*

To play a character [Fagin in *Oliver!*] and to get away from the "stars in the eyes, get the girl thing", that was the most attractive and most satisfying thing that I ever did as an actor. The London Times wrote, "If you're here to see Davy Jones

from The Monkees, forget it. This guy's done his homework."
Now that was tearful![98]

*

I just got two sheets for me to do some voiceovers in a movie, some stuff for a cartoon or a TV animation, so my career has always been moving. I've always been on the go. Not always in the magazines and all that kind of stuff, but I've been a working actor all my life. It doesn't matter if the load is heavier or lighter, I'm still paying the rent. I'm still doing the things I do.[99]

*

It's been a long journey; September [2011] will be my anniversary: fifty years as a professional entertainer! My first gig was in the early sixties on the BBC Radio and BBC Television, and theatre, Broadway, West End of London, so it's been a long journey but I'm still having great fun.[100]

*

SAM S. **SHUBERT** THEATRE

22 W. Monroe St.   DIRECTION MESSRS. SHUBERT   Chicago 3

DAVID MERRICK and DONALD ALBERY

present

LIONEL BART'S

OLIVER!

**Book, Music and Lyrics by
LIONEL BART**

Freely adapted from Dickens' "Oliver Twist"

starring

JUDY BRUCE   ROBIN RAMSAY

with

ALAN CROFOOT   DANNY SEWELL
BRAM NOSSEN   JOHN CALL   DAWNA SHOVE

RONNIE & DAVID
KROLL   JONES

RUTH MAYNARD   JOHN MIRANDA

Directed by
PETER COE

Designed by
SEAN KENNY

Orchestrations by   *Musical Director*   *Technical Supervisor*   *Lighting by*
ERIC ROGERS   **ROBERT McNAMEE**   **IAN ALBERY**   **JOHN WYCKHAM**

Talk About David Jones

When I was young, I had these three silly ambitions: I said I wanted to ride a camel, walk a tightrope and make a million dollars. Well I did all three of them.[101]

*

My mother was instrumental in giving me the softer side to my character.[102]

*

I [had a] "security" pillow — which I took with me everywhere until I was about five years old.[103]

*

My favorite game as a child was playing Doctor. I would examine the patients and always diagnose that they had some terrible plague. Then, of course, I would operate and save their lives.[104]

*

I didn't have many toys because most of the money my father made went for the essential things we lived on. So, I made most of my own toys. I did a lot of wood carving. I made a train, a pair of stilts, a bow and arrow (which was my favorite) and an Indian tomahawk. I also would pretend I was a Knight (as in "in shining armor," only I had no armor) and ran about dueling with all my friends.[105]

*

When I was 13 I fell in love with my science teacher. She was very pretty and I would ask her embarrassing questions in front of the class.

She would get very red and say, "I'll tell you after class, Mr. Jones."

So I got to stay after class and talk to her.[106]

*

Well, when you first start smoking it's in the toilet. My father used to call me Wood-buying Willie. I used to sit in the toilet and I didn't really smoke, I used to puff on a cigarette when I was about twelve years old. The smoke would come underneath the door, which was in the backyard, and they used to call me Wood-buying Willie.[107]

*

I thought about [being famous] at school. I used to write my name — David Jones — almost the same autograph! Don't ask me why, kids go through these fantasies.

I used to tell kids, "When I get older, I'm going to America, you know! That's where I'm going, America."[108]

*

Uprooting from England and moving to America at a very young age was not really a big risk for me, because I had a job. The producer from America came over, saw me in the part [of the Artful Dodger in *Oliver!*], thought I'd be better for the American audience than the kid that was doing it; I replaced him in Canada, and [then] I was in Broadway.

It was a tough thing for me because they broke down at Christmas — there was no show on Christmas Day or the next day — and I didn't know what to do. I was fifteen years old, and I just sat on the pavement outside the theatre at the stage door eating a bacon, lettuce and tomato sandwich. I was going, "What am I doing here? This is ridiculous. I want to go home."

The same thing when I left home at fourteen and went into the stables; I cried a couple of times. But you've got to grow up and you've got to move on. So, [moving to America] wasn't a risk professionally. *Personally* it was a risk, because I had to be a grown-up before most kids have left school, and I was pretty much on my own.

It was kinda scary, but then I got into the American life.[109]

*

People stared at me when I walked down the street [in New York]. I couldn't understand it, then I realised that I had long hair, which suited my role as the Artful Dodger, but all the American males had crew cuts. Everything was so big, so different from England. I'd never eaten a steak in England but in America I had it every meal for a month, including breakfast.[110]

*

The Davy Jones in *The Monkees* pretty much was who I was, as far as the tone of my voice, the dialogue, and the things that I said. I used to turn their dialogue around a little bit to suit me because I would interpret it differently.[111]

*

I'm just a caricature of myself really: Davy Jones from *The Monkees*.[112]

*

When we started filming [*The Monkees*], there were these three six-footers and then there was little me.

Every time they went to do a floor shot, it was like, "Where is he?"

So they used to say, "A man-maker for Davy!"

I hated that.

And they'd bring a box and I'd stand on it.[113]

*

I used to have this hairdresser, Sally, on the set, and she used to turn my hair underneath at the back. I was the first one to have that sort of long hair at the back, short hair on top stuff. I remember seeing Bowie down at the Auditorium in Santa Monica, California, and all of a sudden, he had the extended Davy Jones haircut. And Bowie, his real name is David Jones. He had to change it because I already had that one locked up with the unions. But I don't think it hurt his career. I think he did quite well, thank you very much.[114]

*

But I'm not out to compete or to copy, I just do what I've always done, and good, bad, or indifferent, I *was* the guy that made David Bowie change his name! There's more Davy Jones's in England than there is of any other name, so Bowie had to change it. I actually saw him in '73 in Santa Monica, California, when he was doing Ziggy Stardust, and it broke my heart, and I was so jealous when he did a duet with Bing Crosby.[115]

*

I was watching the show the other day, *The Monkees* TV show, with one of my daughters, and I was doing my little Davy Jones dance, and my daughter says to me, "Dad, why are you dancing like Axl Rose?"

I said, "Axl Rose? Been there, done that, got the t-shirt."

That's how I used to keep my waist so slim, you see, all that little Davy Jones dancing there, backwards and forwards. I guess I should do it a little bit more often these days.[116]

*

This guy Justin Bieber? He stole my haircut! And that Axl Rose, he stole my dance! Plus, I'm the guy that made David Bowie change his name.[117]

*

The reason that I was a teen idol was because I wasn't threatening. I'm a little guy and I'm not gonna jump on you and hurt you. It's funny, because there were a lot of guys who were my fans too, like a brotherly thing. The girls felt that way too. It wasn't a sexual thing with The Monkees, not the fans that were looking at *me*, anyway.

When you become successful on a TV show like *The Monkees*, you become better looking, more intelligent, bigger in every way than you really are. The hardest thing was my family, because they were bombarded by newsmen. When I visited my father, newsmen would rent a room in the house across the street, where they could wait there for me to come home and take pictures, knowing full well I was in the country and I'd be there. I had to climb over the back fence in a woman's dress and a scarf to get to my house.

The fans knocked a wall down in front because they wanted the bricks. There's some girl in England who's got one of my bricks: "This is from Davy Jones' wall!" It meant something to her and that's why she kept it.[118]

*

I remember going home to Manchester, going home to England. This is very, very clear in my mind. I did dress up like a girl, and I went over the back fence.

They used to steal the bricks from the wall at the front of the house. There was half a garden wall![119]

*

If I don't go to Palm Springs, my Saturdays are spent playing golf. I love, love, love golf! It's fascinating and relaxing — even though I am not very good at it yet.

I decided not to move from my house in the Hollywood Hills, so say goodbye to my idea of a ranch in Malibu! I really do like my present home, so I am not upset a bit about not moving. In fact, I am very happy. My garage — which used to be full of mail — has been cleared out and I have made my own personal recording studio, where I can sing, play and then listen to my own playbacks.

The interior of the house, by the way, is being completely redecorated — by me. The main color I am using is my favorite color — which is blue. I guess you could call the furniture style a combination of Olde English and Modern Comfortable!

All is not peaceful at *chez Jones*, however. Recently, some girls broke into the garage and, for some unknown reason, released the brake on my Cadillac. The Cadillac rolled down the cement drive and crashed into a pole! The front was dented and all the windows were broken.

As a result of this incident, I am forced to build an electric fence around my property and to install electric gates with a speaker box on them — so that I can find out, in advance, who is entering the grounds. What a drag![120]

*

People always expect you to be jumping out of a Rolls Royce and being in the papers for drunk and disorderly or sleeping around. I'm a family man with three kids, and I got a new addition coming in June (1988). I own property in a quiet little town of Pennsylvania. I've got an apartment in Hollywood. I own a place in Australia. I've got a farm in England where I breed horses. It's very difficult over the years when people say. "Oh, you're making a comeback." When you say *comeback*, it sounds like you've been somewhere. I've been so active.[121]

*

Show business is full of bad behavior. When I go into a place, the wardrobe lady will ask, "Do you have something to iron, Mr. Jones?"

And I'll say, "No, thank you. My name's *David*. I've ironed all my clothes."

And by the time we're done, I'm telling jokes and everyone is laughing.

We try to set a good example. I am the same person when I leave this house as I am on the stage, wherever it might be.

I've got nothing else to be.[122]

*

I think best [when I'm under pressure], when somebody's on my back. When I'm in a corner of a room I fight the best. I fight the hardest because I want to get out of the corner.[123]

*

I was always that feisty little guy going, "Are you talking to me?" and picking fights. I suppose I felt an insecurity.[124]

*

Don't tell me I'm a goody-two-shoes because I still like a fight, okay, all right? Don't mess around with me, because I'll kick your ass, okay? I handle twelve-hundred pound horses, okay? It's not something that I look to, but I'm the kind of guy that would step in if I see somebody pulling somebody around, or when children are being treated less than kind. I've had confrontations with mothers and fathers in supermarkets! It gets a little drastic.[125]

*

Actually, I am a very shy person.[126]

*

I am an entertainer: I love to entertain. I love to show off. I did it in the school play, I did it in church, I did it all over the place. I don't always want to be the centre of attention when I walk into a room – sometimes I just want to be quiet and I want to listen.[127]

*

I have a life that's quite normal. I'm on the darts team at the local pub. I'm pretty good actually! You'd be quite surprised — a lot of guys have to shoot "down"… I have to shoot straight up, it's right in my eye-line![128]

*

For the most part I try to be unknown and anonymous. As soon as the curtain comes down I become this middle aged man with responsibilities and recreational outlets that everybody else has.[129]

*

I bought an old house in Pennsylvania in the Eighties and people think I'm in the Witness Protection Program. I'm there because I'm unknown, anonymous, and that's what I like to be.

And then I go and I find [very enthusiastic audiences].[130]

*

It's strange being me. All my life I've had people do everything for me, but here, for the last twelve years, I've done what everyone else does. Go to the PO box. Buy some eggs at the grocery store.

[Then] Saturday, I go to Pasadena and play for thousands of people.[131]

*

As soon as the curtain comes down, that's the little guy I become. Onstage it's a whole different story, I enjoy it so much.[132]

*

I believe when an audience goes to see an entertainer, they go to see some of the things that they remember the artist for. So when I go out there and I perform "Daydream Believer" for instance and I see the audience singing: "*I could hide…*" and they're singing these words — and this was almost forty years ago — it doesn't matter whether you're performing to one person, a hundred people, or a hundred thousand, I still give the same performance, personally, because I want to be as good as they want me to be.[133]

*

I'm not offended when David Letterman votes me the number one, the number three, and the number ten tambourine player in the world. Whether it's tongue-in-cheek or whatever, you've got to live with these things. You learn to live with certain things that happen because not everybody knows everything about you and what you do.[134]

*

I work, travel and play. It's kind of funny performing in Disney World for families one night, and Vegas the next before a lot of drunken executives.[135]

*

I still want to be excited by a conversation or an idea. My greatest thrill is the unknown.[136]

*

I just want people to view me in a different way. I mean you're not sure when you're going to see friggin' Davy Jones from The Monkees, know what I mean? What's he gonna do, get stars in his eyes and kiss the girl or whatever?[137]

*

You've got to keep a naivety in in the business as well, because otherwise you get a reputation of being somebody that you're really not; you can't act being *yourself*, you can't act being David Jones, this *is* David Jones! I'm sorry, there you go. Maybe I talk too much, maybe I don't talk enough, maybe I don't laugh enough, maybe I cry too much, but all those things are things that you incorporate into your personality. That's what endears, I think.[138]

*

I quietly do what I do, and I've never been any different about that. Anyone who knows me will tell you that I'm approachable. I'm still the same guy I was. Remember me the way you hoped I'd be, and that's who's talking to you right now.[139]

*

Remember me the way you hoped I'd be. That's what I say to myself.[140]

*

I mean, I've been Davy Jones from The Monkees for almost forty years now.

Live with *that* one!

Ah, it's not so bad.[141]

Talk About Education

Experience is an efficient teacher. School teaches you off the blackboard; life teaches you firsthand through people.

I have learned more through people in my six years *out* of school than I would have in ten years *in* school. This job is important to me. I left school at fourteen. That was a big mistake. I regret it. This is the only work I know. I'm clean. I'm neat. I work because I want a job.[142]

*

I've already got a good start on an acting career — in fact, I've got more than a start. But I look at my friends that are just getting out of school — they're twenty-one or twenty-two — and they still don't know what they're going to do. It seems a waste because with all their schooling, chances are they'll wind up having to buck for a job against someone's son — and the son will get the job.[143]

*

You have to rely on developing talents *within* yourself, lots of abilities, and then use education to push yourself even farther. I mean, you can't learn everything from a book. I want my sons to *do* things, not just study about them. That's a real education.[144]

*

Varna Street School, Openshaw, Manchester.

Talk About Fame

We're all famous somewhere, aren't we? I find people so inspiring. A lot of people that never get any gratitude or favour for the things that they do.[145]

*

The Rock and Roll Memorabilia Museum is so great. There'll be two big areas, one will have lots of memorabilia from The Monkees, mostly stuff from The Monkees, and then "Davy Jones's Favourites", people I've admired over the years.

I'm not gonna wait to be inducted into The Rock and Roll Hall of Fame, I'm gonna build my own! It's only a man-made thing anyway. No, I'm not bitching about that. I'm saying they missed out, because there's a lot of bands that started out listening to The Monkees, and they're already in the Rock and Roll Hall of Fame.[146]

*

When I tell people I have a memorabilia museum, they say, "Oh, is that because you're not in the Rock and Roll Hall of Fame?"

No. [The Rock and Roll Hall of Fame is] run by a gentleman, he owns it, he put the idea together, and I think he owned Rolling Stone Magazine. He never liked The Monkees. It's a voting situation where you're supposed to have a board that votes people in. It's a preference to the ones that run it. If I was not a Monkee, and I was a Monkee *fan* (as I am a Monkee fan!), and I didn't see anything there on The Monkees, I'd be wondering why they weren't there, because the people don't see the politics of that.

All those bands from the sixties — The Beach Boys, The Association, The Turtles — all these different bands had studio musicians [The Wrecking Crew] playing their music. Obviously the third album The Monkees did, *Headquarters*, we did our own stuff, but it's not the end of the world. It would be wonderful to have the acknowledgement of being in the Rock and Roll Hall of Fame, but at the same time it's not something that I'm going to lose any sleep over. And I'm proud of the people that are in there, and that's what America is about: success. Booker T. Washington said: "Success is not to be measured by the position you reach in life, but by the obstacles you overcome to reach that success."

There's many, many fans that are interested in The Monkees going in the Rock and Rock hall of Fame because they take it personally that we're *not*. I can't take it personally anymore because I know what I do, and I say, quite tongue-in-cheek, flippantly, that tonight at the Canyon Club, whoever comes in tomorrow better be bloody good! They had better be good, I'm telling you now, because I'm going to just go kick some ass out there tonight! I've got the songs, I've got the band, and I've got the support. They're not coming here to *test* me, they're coming here to be *entertained* and that's why I'm here, is to entertain people.[147]

*

Why do we find these young kids that are in the movies or in music or whatever coming out of the clubs at two or three in the morning, shooting the finger at the paparazzi? Go to Denny's, for christ's sake! Go to Denny's if you don't want to be bothered. Just go and perform, the curtain comes down, you're finished, that's it.[148]

*

Obviously, I'm a big fan of the [entertainment] business, so anybody that's had any success at all, or has any recognition, or has been able to accomplish certain things, I know how hard it is to do, so I have tremendous respect. It's just a very, a *very,* tough thing to deal with. It's a very lonely life, being in the business.

You know, you do a concert, we play to thousands of people, and then you go home to the hotel, and you close the door, and on goes the TV, and you eat potato chips. Or if you want to go to the bar, or you want to go out partying, you can, but you've got to be on the bus the next morning, so it kind of gets difficult.

I can understand and identify with people that are in the limelight, you know, because I've sort of been a recognizable person for many years now, and it's not easy sometimes.[149]

*

It's a responsibility, being an entertainer, because people do look at you. So there are certain times when it gets too much for you and you feel like, "Cor, I just want to do something *naughty!*"

But I think, once you're in the public eye, you've got to watch what you do. You have to be very professional and you have to be aware of what other people's feelings might be toward you, so you just don't do certain things that are gonna offend. And sometimes it's not always right for you, but it's right for the total overall picture, you know? You've got to be careful what you do.[150]

*

You really can't give advice to anybody. I always to try to look at myself — and hopefully the people will look at themselves — as an *individual*: although they are a songwriter, although they're a technician, a cameraman, whatever it might be, everybody does it a little *differently.* There's techniques that you've got to apply to every sort of performance. But nobody does what Davy Jones does, nobody does what Jack Keller, or Tommy Boyce does, nobody does what Micky Dolenz, or Peter Tork, or Mike Nesmith does, they are individuals in the same sort of business.[151]

*

Just always try to be positive, and also be a good listener, because sometimes in show business you can know *too* much, which also puts people off.[152]

*

My wife worked for a company called Chrysalis Records in England, I think about 15 years ago, and she designed a t-shirt while she was there. And this t-shirt was just a t-shirt but it looked like a tuxedo. Now that thing, a couple of years later, went all over the world. Now she designed it for the company, and she was a secretary in the office, and she made her

$120 a week. The t-shirt made multi-multi-millions of dollars all the way around the world. She'll never have a name on the t-shirt, but she did design it.

In the business, there are some nasty people and there are some nice people. And it's far easier to be nice than nasty, so you be careful who you step on and who you insult and who you take on, because, as they say, you meet them on the way down as well as on the way up.[153]

*

I know what you've got to have in show business… You've got to be a good listener and a good talker.[154]

*

You've got to have a good confidante. My brother-in-law is mine. I've gone through all kinds of cheating people in my life who've stolen money from me, and I walk away. I think, "More fool me". But I'm not gonna walk away from this, because I wanna work with these guys, and I like working with them, and why shouldn't I?[155]

*

The intensity and spotlight was fantastic. It still is fantastic. The people that remember [The Monkees] — other than when they say I look like Dudley Moore — it went on, and it goes on, and it goes on for all of us. All of the artists here today, we're still working, we're still travelling, we're still doing fairs, and parks, and television shows, and things like that, so we're always in the public eye. If you want to entertain you've got to continue to keep working.[156]

*

The hardest thing for an entertainer to do is to break that mould and all of a sudden become a "regular, normal person". And although you want to have that separation, it's very difficult for people to do that. I have something that I'm able to fact base my emotions on, and that is I have three sisters, and I have relatives, and a family home in England, as well as many people I like, respect, and care about. And same goes for them with me. So I try to separate that.[157]

*

Michael Jackson *can* go shopping in a giant supermarket if he doesn't go Friday night, show up in a limousine, and moonwalk into the store. He's not going to have any trouble if he goes Thursday night, a half-hour before closing, and he's in the cheese aisle.[158]

*

It's kind of interesting when people *don't* recognize me — that kind of feels more weird than anything — and I don't go out of my way to have people recognize me. My voice is very,

very familiar to a lot of people, so it's kind of hard: "I didn't recognize your face, but I recognized your voice."[159]

*

Most careers are fishbowls. Sammy Davis, Jr., Dean Martin, Frank Sinatra, they go up, they go down, and they settle for somewhere in the middle of the bowl, and end up with a long and successful career. And that's what I've got: the most unused recognizable voice in America.[160]

*

That was a really difficult thing to live with [being a teen idol], I didn't really feel any different when I did The Monkees than I did when I did the school play. It was just like a continuation from school, to the broadway stage, to some television appearances on some obscure shows like Ben Casey and The Farmer's Daughter and Bewitched — and then I followed it up in the 90's and 80's with My Two Dads and Scooby Doo Meets Davy Jones, and most recently (one of my greatest appearances) on SpongeBob, which made me a little bit more credible with my grandchildren! (I do have grandchildren.)[161]

*

You know they just voted me the number one teen idol of all time! Beating out Miley Cyrus, and Madonna, and a number of other people. But who's running that? Who's making those predictions?

But I'm very grateful to the career that I've had, and the career that I'm having, and I always look forward to the next performance.[162]

*

Talk About Family

I used to see more of my mother than anyone. All my older sisters passed their scholarships and went on to other schools, but I didn't pass, so I had to go to the school just down the street. Because it was so near our house, I would come home for lunch each day. And how I loved that![163]

*

The rooms were only about 12 by 8, two up, two down. I slept in a room with my three sisters, and my mum and dad were in the other room. Toilet out in the backyard, no bathroom; we washed in the sink.[164]

*

My mother was a very thoughtful and kind person. Everything she did was for my father and us kids. I can remember one Guy Fawkes Day — which is the holiday on November 5th in honor of an old English chap who was beheaded for trying to blow up Parliament. In his honor every street has a big bonfire.

I was about ten years old and my mates and I went down to the railway yard and got a great wooden line from where they were laying tracks, and we tied ropes around it and dragged it all the way home. This was to be our contribution to the street bonfire and we took so long dragging it home we were out way past dark.

When I walked in the house my mother belted me, and she yelled, "Get in here!" She was really mad that I was out past dark. So I was feeling very bad, but I had to come downstairs to take my bath. When I came down she had hot chocolate all ready and the bath steaming hot.

We had no bathroom in our house so there I sat in a tin basin in the kitchen holding hot chocolate in my hands while she scrubbed me down. That scene was very typical of my mother — she had scolded me for doing something wrong and ten minutes later all was forgotten and she was taking care of me once more.[165]

*

I remember sitting in that old tub saying to her, "I'm going to buy you a big house someday, with a lovely big bath."

She'd laugh and say, "Sure you are… but not if you don't pass your eleven class!"

But I never got to buy her that house. And I never did pass that eleven class.[166]

*

Because my mother was often ill, all us kids would help out. I used to go shopping for her, or I'd run errands she'd need done. On the days we'd go out to the country I'd always gather a bouquet of flowers, which she loved.[167]

*

Sometimes [my father's railway club] would have special women's cricket matches. My mother would never play, but she was always the umpire. And she'd always cheat and let the women win! It was so funny, she'd make up her own set of rules! She really made it fun and we'd be up in the stands cheering away and laughing hysterically.[168]

*

Dad didn't want me to spend my whole life like he did and have nothing to show for it. He wanted me to go out and make some money so I wouldn't have to worry when I got to his age. He would even send me spending money while I was training. Most fathers just want their sons to bring their wages home. That's how it happens in England — you give your wages to your parents and they give you an allowance. It's the proper thing to do.[169]

*

My father never earned more than thirty dollars a week. But he never made us feel poor. He did the best he could. The neighbors were charging things like fridges, fancy furnishings and such, but my dad saved what little he could so that each year he could take us kids for a holiday at St. Anne's near Blackpool. No one 'round us could do that, but my dad saw to it. A million dollars couldn't repay him.[170]

*

The house had an outdoor toilet and no bathroom at all. I remember I had to wash myself in the kitchen sink. We all had to do that. Some of my relatives still do. But it wasn't like we were poor in a rich neighbourhood. Everyone was poor in Higher Openshaw. Dad had to struggle to buy us clothes and food, but so did every other dad in the area. Every year we used to go away on a two week holiday. We were the only kids in the neighbourhood who got to do that. We used to go to a place called St. Annes, near Blackpool, but cheaper. Everybody else was busy buying furniture and new television and all that, but my father was busy making sure we had a good time.[171]

*

I've got three sisters and we had it a little hard, but we always went away for two weeks holiday every year. You *never* find my dad sitting in the pub; the money he would have spent for the beer he would save and take us away, to just get us out for a while, get away from the smoke, the whole thing.[172]

*

Vacations were always very important to my mum and dad. While other parents were going to the local pub to have a few beers, my folks were sitting home watching TV or something and saving their money. Consequently, they saved enough money in order for us to have a two week holiday each year.

We'd usually go to St. Ann's Beach and we'd always stay at the same place, which was right next to the fire station. We loved that because it was so exciting to see the big red engines go racing out.

I'll never forget the place where we always stayed: Mrs. Brown's boarding house.

We had such fun along the beach in those days. We never had enough money to go to the amusement parks, so we had fun just running up and down the sand hills at St. Ann's.

We had a great time, too, when we'd go for walks with my dad through the park. I can remember it had big outdoor bird cages and we used to love seeing all the different birds.

It was always a big thrill for us to go to the park. We'd sit on this one bench along one particular walk where my father made his pools — like the Irish Sweepstakes. In England they have a pool every week. Anyway, once he won and got 280 pounds (that's about 700 dollars) and we got all rigged out in clothes and my dad kept about five quid (that's about 12 dollars) for himself.[173]

*

No one knew I was coming home [for Christmas 1966]. I had written and told them I wasn't sure if I could come home or not. Then I wrote and said I *couldn't* make it.

I knocked on the door and my sister answered. She looked at me and as soon as she did, she started to cry. I told her to be quiet and I walked through the hallway to the living room and my father nearly fainted.[174]

*

During my Christmas [1966] visit home, I spent ten days with my dad. Three of these were spent recuperating from a bout with the flu, which hit me just about the time my feet hit English soil! For Christmas, I redecorated my dad's home. By the way, my dad, who (as some of you may know) was under the weather for quite a while, is now feeling just fine. He has gotten the roses back in his checks and is as fit as a fiddle, if you'll pardon a silly expression. Needless to say, we all enjoyed a warm and wonderful Yuletide together.[175]

*

They actually asked me to play my father in [*The Daydream Believers Movie*], which is kind of interesting. That would've been a kick.[176]

*

When I bought my dad a house in Manchester in 1967 for £3,700, [£85,823.17 today] he said he was not moving out of his terrace. He did not want to have a mortgage.

I told him I was paying for it *all*.

That is all he ever wanted: stability, his house and car paid for. Nothing was bought on the never never.[177]

*

He [Basil Foster] was like a second father to me. I've always confided in him and tried to do right by him. He lived in one of my homes in Florida, and is now in this care facility [*in Palm City, for which Davy paid all fees*]. He's as stubborn as ever, but the staff here are excellent. They take good care of him and keep an eye on him, and I take him out to see the horses at the barn when I can. He's still showing me how to long-rein horses, still telling me what to do.[178]

*

I love kids, because I can look them straight in the eye.[179]

*

I'm really looking forward to having a family someday. I want to have at least four kids, maybe six. But I'll adopt a lot of kids also. A lot of kids need adopting. I want my own children, because every man wants his own child, but I could be happy just adopting kids. I would love them just as much.[180]

*

Would I be a strict father? That all depends. If I had a little girl, then I'd be a strict father, because I know what I'm like.[181]

*

I've got lots of ideas about how to raise my sons. When they're fifteen, I want them to decide what they want to do with their lives — which way they want to go. And they've *got* to know what they want to do for a profession by the time they're twenty-one years old. They can't be still going to school. They've got to finish before that if it means taking all sorts of summer courses and things.[182]

*

I've often wondered why I'm so popular with children. I mean, whenever I get stopped and asked for an autograph by a crowd, there are always more kids among *my* fans than for Mike or Peter or Micky.

I think it's because I'm younger looking than the rest of the guys — or any pop singers, for that matter. In fact, there's never been any pop singers that have been as successful as The Monkees and as *young*. There are lots of Bobby Vees and people like that, but they aren't as young as I am. I'm older age-wise, of course, but I'm younger *looking*, and that means a lot. It's as if the kids know they can sit down and talk to me and I can talk on their level. They don't immediately think, "He's a lot older than I am…" because I don't *look* a lot older. They think that, wow! I'm one of them, and they can talk to me like they would a just slightly older brother or friend.[183]

*

L ooking at Christian [Nesmith], it makes me think ahead to when I get married. Straightaway I plan to adopt some kids and have some of my own. I'll have lots of my own — four of my own, and then I want to adopt at least four more, so I'll have eight kids — maybe more. I really dig large, close families!

I especially want to have three girls and one boy of my own. That's because my dad had three girls and a boy and I watched how he brought us all up and I figure I can do the same thing.[184]

*

I love my horses. They come over to me, and they nuzzle their heads by my arm.

[My wife] Jessica asked me, "Why they do that?"

And I told her, "It's all about touch and feel and sound. They're like children."

And speaking of children, one of my daughters just won the Class in Pebble Beach on one of the race horses that I gave to her. She was competing against million dollar horses. I was so proud of her.[185]

*

W hen you're the father of boys, you worry. When you're the father of girls you *pray*. For I was once a boy.[186]

*

I have four daughters. All girls.[187]

*

I have other things that I do. I've been married twice, I have four daughters, all girls, so I try to spend as much time as I can with them, you know, summer holidays. Everybody's got their own lives.[188]

*

To have my grandson here with me especially, my daughters as well, it's very important quality time, and this was another quality moment.[189]

*

When you become successful, you become more intelligent, you become better looking, more articulate, all these things that you're *not*. My kids know all about me; they know my weaknesses, they know my strengths, and they support me in both of those things.[190]

*

I ride out everyday. I have a couple of hunters that I keep, and with my children we enter the summer shows, and the gymkhana, and things like that — all things that dads do with their daughters… and I enjoy it, it's a thing we can all share together as a family. My wife doesn't like it too much because I told her that, next to my horses, I love her the most! So she wasn't too pleased with that.[191]

*

It's lonely when people love the version of you on stage, but I found peace when I was just Davy — mucking about in the garden, helping my kids with homework.[192]

*

I too am married once again and have a three year old daughter Jessica No 3 girl. She's a rascal and only comes when she wants to,. has me in the palm of her hand, just like the first two who are now 16 & 13 — time flies — I keep two horses and expect a foal mid march no me personally I add — Anyway loads of things going on and I should be back in the west end this year, we'll see —

All the best to you & yours

David J.

Talk About Fans

Dear *Tiger Beat* Readers,

I picked up the last *Tiger Beat* and I was reading the letters from all of you when I came across one from Georgia Palmer criticizing me for letting pictures run of me with some of the girls I date. Georgia felt that I was hurting my fans by doing this.

Letter in Tiger Beat

I'm really getting sick and tired of hearing how much Davy loves his fans and wouldn't do anything to hurt them. I know of about four girls who wrote in and said it breaks their hearts to see Davy with other girls. But just think how many beautiful girls you've seen Davy with in pictures!

Do you ever see Peter, Micky or Mike with girls in pictures? No, because they care if their fans get hurt or jealous. In my opinion Davy loves to see his fans get hurt and that's why he probably just loves to have lots of pictures of him with girls in Tiger Beat! Down with Davy!

I was so upset that I decided the only thing I could possibly do was write a letter in reply. I thought about what I should say all day during filming and that night when I got home. I wondered if maybe I *was* hurting my fans by being photographed with my girlfriends — and even those girls I *don't* date. Finally, I just couldn't decide what I should do, or what I should say, so I got on the phone and called two of my best friends and asked them what they thought I should do.

They were no help at all! One thought I should go ahead and continue letting fans know who I date and where I go, and the other thought that I should just withdraw from print where this part of my life is concerned.

That night I couldn't sleep because I had visions of some of my fans standing at the foot of my bed, crying and saying I was hurting them, just like they sometimes do at concerts when we perform. It was awful! I felt terrible that I, Davy Jones, could hurt people so badly when I didn't mean to at all. I'd almost made up my mind to quit being so open about my private life when the phone rang and it turned out to be a fan who had somehow gotten my number and wanted to talk.

Ordinarily, I would have been very upset that a fan — someone who thinks of themself as a friend — would call me in the middle of the night just to talk, when they know that I have to get up early to film.

But this night, I didn't mind a bit. I don't know what her name was or where she lived or what she looked like, but she helped me make my big decision, and right now, I'd like to thank her.

You see, the first thing she asked me was what I was doing, and what my house looked like, and finally, after a while, she asked me who I was dating, and what kind of girls I like, and who I was going out with.

Well, I couldn't keep it in, and I started pouring out my story and my problem over what sort of a decision to make. I had almost decided to become a recluse about my private life.

"But Davy," she said, "you're one of the few people who let their fans know what they're doing. I'd much rather know who you are dating, and what you are doing, than have to sit around and wonder whether you're married, or sitting home unhappily watching television every night because you are lonesome!"

Then she told me a story about how she watched The Monkees when we first came on television and how she used to lie awake nights because she thought I didn't have anyone in the world who cared about me. All she had read said that my family was in England, and that I lived alone, or with friends like Mike sometimes, and she really thought that I must be one of the loneliest people in the world. She said that sometimes she'd sit at the dinner table at her home and look around at her parents and her brothers and sisters and she'd almost break into tears because she wanted to invite me home so that I could share some of her happiness.

I forgot to ask her what she was doing talking on the phone at midnight, but I'm glad she called because I needed someone to talk to and she helped me make my decision.

You see, by the time I had hung up the telephone, I knew that what I've been doing — sharing my experiences with all of you — is right, and that I should continue doing so.

I don't mean to hurt anyone, but think how much it would be hurting me to have to quit going out with girls whose company I enjoy. There wouldn't be any such thing as going out and *not* let pictures be printed, because someone is always there with a camera, and a performer can't say anything about whether the pictures get printed or not. That's all part of freedom of the press.

And if I quit going out, I really would be unhappy because I don't have any family and I don't have time to make a lot of close friends and the few really close friends that I do have often make plans on their own. So I'd wind up spending a lot of time by myself.

But most importantly, if I quit having pictures taken of myself and my girlfriends, I'd feel that I was shutting you out of a big part of my life. I wouldn't be honest and I don't think it would be fair. I want you to share my life and my happiness; and I think that the mark of a mature fan is someone who can accept that I do have my own life to lead. I can't be an actor both on — and off — the stage or the screen or the television set.

I hope this will help explain to all of you why I allow pictures to be taken of me with girls I date. After all, I think it would be fun to see pictures of you having a good time with someone you like. I want everyone to be happy!

With lots of love to all of you,

David Jones[193]

*

I can't begin to say how many fan letters came in back then. In the office, the mail that came in was always ten to one for me. Over the last couple of years I have gotten an average of 2,000 letters a week from fans.[194]

*

There was these two beautiful young girls, Patty and Rhonda, from Phoenix, and crossing the street they'd got run over. They were carrying their Monkee albums, and they'd said they wanted to see Davy Jones. And so I flew off to Phoenix, Arizona, and I met with them, and then I kept going back, time after time. I met a couple of nice people there. Tiff and Claire, an old prospector in a cowboy hat in the desert there, you know, went to visit him a lot, too. So I was enriched by the experience[195]

*

I was just walking in here today, into the [TV Studio] building, and a lady [freezes in shock].

And I said, "You're right, it is." And she was pregnant, and she's with this guy, and so I put my arms out, "Give us a hug, it's been ages since I saw you!"

I don't get it. But if that's a memory and if that's an occasion, I'm not gonna pass it up.[196]

*

The reason I do a radio station, or I go to a television station is because I want those people that are *not* coming to that show to see me, because they haven't seen me in a long time. They think I'm dead![197]

*

This guy comes up to me in the hotel room. He said, "Um, my daughter, she's fourteen years old, she *loves* you! What do you think about that?"

I said, "How old are *you*?"

He says, "Forty-two."

I said, "So am I." I said, "What do you think about your dad?"

She says, "I like him."

I said, "You *love* him?"

She said, "Yeah."

I said, "Well, she loves me, too. That's okay."

It's a different thing, isn't it? When I look back at those times and I see — obviously it's happening that kids are now watching The Monkees again and buying the records and playing the records and having fan clubs and doing all this stuff — it all depends what you think about it. I'm very proud of The Monkees and I wouldn't at all disappoint your wife if she was to tell me about that time that she was feeling close to me. I wouldn't say, "Well, I don't want to talk about it!" I would discuss it, because it was a *time* for me, growing up, too. And if you've got something that you can share, I think that's the main thing. I think that's what The Monkees were all about; we weren't a threat to anybody's boyfriends or anything like that, it was apple pie and ice cream, you know? And cutesy.[198]

*

I get letters all the time. You can't even believe how much time we spend with emails and with fan mail, and all the rest of the stuff. We read it. We don't just throw it away.[199]

*

People are nervous enough and they don't really know. In the middle of all this, somebody can come and talk to us, as if you're just another man. I mean that's like familiarity that you can't buy. That makes me feel good that they feel so causal about the idea. It's sort of empowering.[200]

*

I'm approachable — as far as the kids are concerned — I'm not threatening, I'm not a bearded monster, I'm not an unapproachable person, and I think the humanity and the humility (although they say humility breeds contempt!) You've gotta humble yourself sometimes to situations, and if somebody mentions The Monkees to me, I say, "Yeah, right, that was a great time!" And [if they ask where's Micky, Mike and Peter,] I'll make a joke, I'll go: "Oh, they're in the Actor's Home in Hollywood. I went to see them before I left; I said, 'Do you know who I am?' And Peter said, 'Ask the nurse, she'll tell you.'" So I make fun of that whole situation, and I love The Monkees memories that people have and share with me all the time.[201]

*

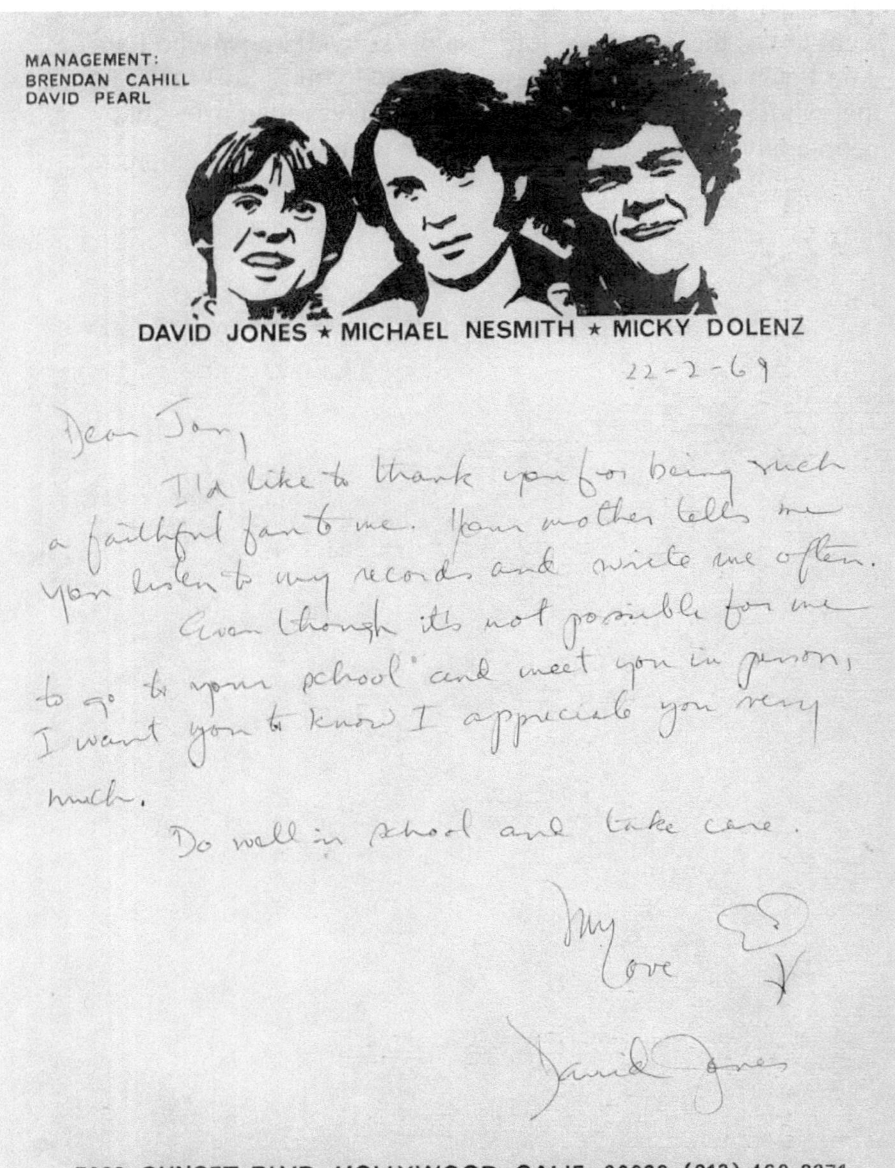

22-2-69

Dear Jan,

I'd like to thank you for being such a faithful fan to me. Your mother tells me you listen to my records and write me often.

Even though it's not possible for me to go to your school and meet you in person, I want you to know I appreciate you very much.

Do well in school and take care.

My Love

David Jones

Talk About Fear

The peak of fear only lasts about two seconds. And if you think about what's going to happen, it just makes it worse. If you worry about something it just magnifies the problem.

I'm never really worried to the point of fear. I just take things lightly. I figure if something is going to happen, it's going to happen.[202]

*

I'd love someone to get in my shoes one day; when I get up on a racehorse in the morning, and my legs are up in my chin, and I I'm galloping along, and I'm looking about, and there's a couple of guys alongside, and we're going forty miles an hour, and you're sitting pinned up on top of a horse; it's a thrilling feeling! It's an amazing adrenaline rush. But you know, three or four or five horses a morning, doing this, the odds of you having some sort of mistake — this is an animal, and it's traveling.

It's just the fear of the unknown, this is what people have.

I love it. I love the unknown. This is what I live for. I wanna say to myself: there's got to be something *more*, there's gonna be something *more*![203]

Talk About Food

My mum was an excellent cook. Steak and kidney pie was her best dish, and Sunday dinners were always a special treat. Every Sunday we'd go to church and we'd have dinner around two in the afternoon. It was always something special, like leg of lamb or roast with roast potatoes. And it was always delicious![204]

*

One time I had a housekeeper, a nice lady who did all my cooking for me. So I felt like the Lord of the Manor — all that "Dinner is served" stuff and that kind of thing. But I found I was nipping into the kitchen between meals and knocking up a meal for myself. So, I bought cookery books and tried more exotic dishes and my mates thought it was good, so I decided I could get along without a resident housekeeper.

I haven't poisoned anybody yet, so I can't be too bad. I've got the proper chef's hat, too — it's just about as tall as I am.[205]

*

I went to a restaurant and I asked the man, "How do you prepare your chicken?"

He says, "We come straight out and tell them: 'You're gonna *die*!'"[206]

*

Baked Zucchini with Noodles (On "Country Kitchen" with Florence Henderson)

Sauté the chopped zucchini. Zucchini is very good. I love veggies. Put that in a bowl.

The next thing we need is the garlic. Add that in there. An apple a day keeps the doctor away — a garlic a day keeps *everybody* away!

Then we get the mushrooms, we put the mushroom in here, ya see. I love mushrooms; I had a friend that had some bad luck with mushrooms. You can eat most mushrooms, and you can go into the woods and take them. But you've got to be very careful. There are one or two you can't eat. A friend of mine's wife died from eating poison mushrooms. Very bad luck. And he had a second wife. She died from a fractured skull. She wouldn't eat the mushrooms. (I'm not a chauvinist, I swear, just a cheap joke, I'm sorry, I had to throw it in.)

And then we add the [tin of chopped] tomatoes.

The next thing is bread crumbs. Now you have to get these in fast or otherwise the birds will get them. In they go, brown bread crumbs. Stir it all around. This is lovely.

When I'm on the road working I do a lot of cooking. It's very difficult because most hotels don't have the kitchens. You've got to go to sort of apartment hotels, and they're not very nice. Some of them, the walls are so thin, I open the oven door and some guy from the next room is dipping his bread in my gravy! Thin walls!

Sour cream! Not sour grapes after that joke! Just splash it in there.

Cooking should be a fun thing. It is in our house, anyway. It's an adventure, actually, when I get into the kitchen.

Okay, we got the sour cream, we need some almonds, lovely. Protein is very, very important.

Pasta for me is an energy booster, that's why, for runners, you've really got to get that kind of stuff in there, especially if you're a veggie.

Paprika! Just a nice little spoonful. Keep stirring. The wooden spoon's gotta keep on the move here so you don't bruise the food. Just lightly cook it there, because it's gonna bake in a little while.

And I think next we should put in the zucchini.

It's vey difficult actually cooking with somebody in the kitchen, if you prepare all your gear, if you prepare all your stuff to start off with, I think that's important. And what I do, is I sort of clean up after myself as I go along — with the dishes and the pans.

What we're going to do now is, we're going to put this into the casserole dish, as much of it as we can.

If you're a cockney, you grew up within the sound of the bow bells, which is some bells that go off occasionally in London. I am not a cockney, I'm from Manchester, north country.

I have three sisters. I guess that was pretty big; four kids. I have four daughters of my own. All girls. I love to cook for them but they just eat at different times. But I'm trying to get the younger kids into eating this kind of stuff.

And then you put the [parmesan] cheese on top of that.

I'm gonna put it in the oven; I'm gonna bake it for 30 minutes at maybe 350.

1. Preheat your oven 350'.

2. Sauté zucchini slices in 3/8 cup oil.

3. Remove zucchini; place in large bowl.

4. Add remaining oil to pan.

5. Sauté garlic and mushrooms.

6. Add tomatoes and stir.

7. Stir in bread crumbs, sour cream, almonds and paprika; mix well.

8. Cook 1 min. Remove from heat.

9. Add tomato mixture to zucchini; mix well.

10. Spoon mixture into dish.

11. Sprinkle with cheese and bake 30 min.

12. Serve with noodles.[207]

*

<u>Davy's Aussie Oatmeal Bread</u>

1 ¼ pound butter
⅓ cup dark brown sugar
¼ teaspoon baking soda
2 teaspoons water
1 ½ cups oatmeal
1 teaspoon powdered ginger

Cream the butter; add the sugar and beat until light and fluffy. Dissolve the baking soda in the water and add, stirring well. Add the oatmeal and ginger, mixing well. The mixture should be fairly firm. If necessary, add a little more oatmeal. Knead lightly on a floured surface.

Preheat oven to 300°. Press the mixture into a buttered baking dish, about 8 by 12 inches. The dough should be about ½ inch thick. Bake in a 300° oven for 35 minutes, or until brown on top. Cut into squares while hot (if desired).[208]

*

Davy's Meringue Shells

2 egg whites
⅛ teaspoon cream of tartar
Dash salt
½ cup sugar
½ teaspoon vanilla

Beat egg whites with cream of tartar and salt until stiff but not dry. Add sugar, 1 tablespoon at a time, beating until stiff after each addition. Fold in the vanilla. Heap in rounds or press through a pastry tube onto a baking sheet covered with heavy ungreased paper while making sure that the dough forms a basket shape so that you can put things in it.

Bake in a slow oven (275 F.) 40–60 minutes or until lightly browned.

Remove at once from paper so it won't stick. Makes 18 large meringues.

After the meringue has cooled, there are several things you can do with it.

1. You can add ice cream and chocolate sauce to it.

2. You can cover it with fruit and an appropriate sauce.

3. You can put jam in it and top it with sweet thick cream or a sweet thick cream that has chocolate sauce added to it.

4. You can put a custard in it and top it with either colored or white sweet whipped cream.[209]

*

Davy's "Old Soup"

Ingredients: Any and all veggies that you have in the fridge that are still edible! Make sure the vegetables are chopped fine.

Directions: Heat a large pot with water. Season with salt, pepper and one vegetable bouillon cube. Cut it up, boil it up, and you've got "Old Soup."[210]

*

Davy's Very English Crumpets

2 cakes or packages yeast
½ cup lukewarm water
2 eggs
1 ½ cups lukewarm milk
2 tablespoons melted butter
½ teaspoon salt
1 teaspoon sugar
3 cups sifted flour

Dissolve the yeast in the water. Allow to soften for 5 minutes. Beat the eggs, add the milk, butter, salt, and sugar. Add the yeast mixture and the flour, beating until smooth and well blended.

Cover and set aside in a warm place for 15 minutes.

Preheat oven to 400°. Fill buttered muffin tins about half full. Bake in a 400° oven for 15 minutes.

Serve hot with plenty of melted butter and raspberry jam.[211]

*

Food Glorious Food

David Jones

You are what you eat
I'm Pasta

Talk About The Future

I'm trying to put a memorabilia museum together, and make that also a children's theatre. It's an old Lutheran church that was derelict, abandoned, and we tried to refurbish it with a new roof and 36 new windows, new walls, and all kinds of splendid ideas. Going to the school that was closing down and getting the curtain for the stage. Trying to collect memorabilia from all parts of the state of Pennsylvania. As well as lots of Monkees memorabilia, anyone that was following the Monkees in the sixties — or even now — through Rhino records — they were issuing and have issued and still do issue many, many items, whether it be a lunch box, or whether it be a pencil — they seem to have their merchandise department on the go all the time.[212]

*

I *do* happen to have the drum head that says "DRUM" on it, from the front of Micky's drum, which will be displayed in my Pennsylvania memorabilia museum.[213]

*

Dave [Cassidy] and I did a few shows together, but his show is different than what my show is, and that's good, and I was more thinking about him and I doing a couple of tunes together, and doing some schtick… I thought it would be a wonderful idea for David and I to do something because each time we've been together and performed we've sold everything out. But it hasn't worked out. I didn't do as many dates as I thought I would do, but maybe next year.[214]

*

I'm working on a new musical [that takes place in a small English town at the outbreak of World War II.[215]

*

It's got a great book that I've written, and [a longtime friend and I] collaborated on all the songs as far as the storyline and everything else. It's going to be good.[216]

*

We're also working on a show; it's something like Riverdance. We have an amazing choreographer, someone [my wife] Jess has worked with for over 15 years. Jessica is going to be a big star, and if she's not, she'll always be a star in my eyes.[217]

*

I think when you hear these tunes and see this show, you'll be impressed. We've gone the way of *Hello Dolly* and *Funny Girl* — it's a traditional show. It would be a great idea at this time in my life to direct it, produce it… or maybe I'll just go straight to [Producer] Cameron Mackintosh and say "Here it is. Now what do you think about *that*?"[218]

*

The music is finished, the book is finished. I'll probably direct it, and there's a possibility I'll perform in it.[219]

*

It was a fantastic time in my life [playing the Dodger in the sixties]. I've been working with the other Dodger, the Dodger that took over from me in England, and took over from me in the American production, and we've written a musical, it's called *The Call*. And it's gonna be a great musical because it's got great music, it's a lovely story, and hopefully you'll all come and see that one day. Er… I don't know when that's gonna be… has anyone got about twenty-five million dollars they can lend me?[220]

*

I've just bred some beautiful horses last couple of seasons and ready to go this year — well, next year [2012] — I'm looking forward to competing.[221]

*

I really feel that I've overlooked one area of my performing in theatre, and I would like to see — in the next couple of years — to come back to Broadway. And it has crossed my mind that yes I was nominated for a Tony Award. Well, I want one, okay! And you can't get one unless you're here. So we're talking about different shows right now, and things that could happen for me in the year 2003, or there around, and you've got to do that — opera singers are booked up five years in advance, movie stars have got movies for 2004-2005, that's people putting their trust in you — but you have to have that desire to do that.[222]

*

I would like to do Joel Grey's [Emcee role in] *Caberet*. I would like to be Tony Newley in *Stop the World*, I'd like to do Tommy Steele in *Half a Sixpence*. Just those things that would match my personality. As a sixty-five-year-old man, I can't be doing *Barnum*, balancing on a high wire. It's got to be sensible and it's got to be something that I'm going to enjoy.[223]

*

Look, I've done my career. I'll keep performing and maybe I'll do a movie. Our lives take so many twists and turns; it's hard to say what tomorrow will bring. To be honest, though, I'd rather be here with my horses, or swimming on the beach with Jess. And what I really want is to sit back and, in the next twenty years, see Jess do it. She can act; she's a great actress and an amazing dancer. She has the whole package going.[224]

*

I have people who are talking to me about possible things to do in the near future. My idea would be to continue to do personal appearances as a solo entertainer, and with The Monkees. My book signing is something else that I enjoy doing. Getting out there, and talking to the kids, getting on a piano, playing, singing, playing Monkee music, playing Davy Jones' new album: working title of *Squeal,* it's called. And then I have tours that I have set up, personal tours on my own, going to Australia, going to Japan, touring in England.[225]

*

We went to England and did twelve concerts over there, ending up at the Royal Albert Hall. We sold that one out. Then we came back and ended the first run at the Greek Theatre — that was sold out, too. We had great response to the show. It was probably the best one the three of us have done. It had forty songs in it, songs we pulled off different albums. That was three and a half months of each of our lives. We collectively decided that we should take a break, clear the books and regroup. Now we are talking about how to go about the next phase of it.[226]

*

We did 46 concerts this past year... and it was very successful and it's something that might continue this summer [2012] once again.[227]

*

I hope that [in fifty years from now, when they unearth The Monkees Time Capsule] all the albums will be in there, I hope that *They Made a Monkee Out of Me* will be in there, I hope that they've frozen *me* and they put me in there, and I'll be there when they open it up![228]

*

All the things I've done in show business have been wonderful, but I don't go around: "Oh, I used to be a Monkee!" That's obviously how most people remember Davy Jones, but I want to find something else in my life from this point on. I'm interested in the future, and I have a lot of things in mind so, hey, stay tuned. There'll be more.[229]

Talk About Girls

It's hard to have a girlfriend if you're a Monkee. You may not believe it, but Micky, Peter, and I can't have a simple girl-boy relationship as easily as most of the regular boys in high school.

In the first place, if we should get interested in a certain girl, right away she's up for a lot of publicity and often some very unkind things are said about her in print. She's put down by some fans and critics and all of a sudden the poor girl is getting knocked right and left. Most girls won't put up with this so there goes one more fun relationship out the window.

There's very little time to date when you're a Monkee, as I've said many times before, so it's more likely that you'll meet many different girls and go out on one or two dates without getting serious over anyone. This is the way it has to be for all of us, unless, of course, the girl in our lives is totally understanding about the other demands upon our time.

We've been put down for having too many girls on the set when we work, but I don't think this is quite fair. We enjoy having girls around whether they're fans or personal friends. It's important to us to get a girl's reaction over our songs and performances. And it makes everything more fun. Also, there's a certain excitement when girls are around that just plain isn't there when you have a film crew working all alone without anyone watching.

Since we've been together, Micky, Peter, and I have all had quite a few different girlfriends. With each of these girls we shared a great deal of fun and understanding and we hope that their experiences with us proved valuable in many ways. When we go to choose a wife, it'll be these experiences that help us know when the right person comes along.

The one thing that stands out most in my mind about Mike and Phyllis' marriage is the fact that even though they love each other and are married, Phyllis is still Mike's girlfriend. The fun and excitement of their relationship has never seemed to wear off. I hope this is the way it will be with me when I finally get the chance to marry. In the meantime, I hope all of you will learn to like our choices as girlfriends because they really do make our lives much happier.[230]

*

Wow! There are so many rumors about me and birds that I don't know which one to deny first. I guess we had better start with Lulu. Don't get me wrong. Lulu is a lovely girl — and she really is a good friend of mine — but there is absolutely no romance between us. I have dated her a few times, and when I go to England in May to visit my father I probably will see Lulu and appear on the TV special she will be making then. That is really all there is to it.

Deana Martin: although we do not date anymore, I often drop by the house to say hi to Deana and her family. The Martins are fine people, and I deeply enjoy their company.

The girl named Linda, whom I was dating for a while, is also still a good friend, but there is nothing serious between us. I guess what it comes down to is that your boy, Davy Jones, has an eye for the girls. I dig being with them and I dig dating them, but I also like being single, foot-loose and fancy-free. It is a good way to be — don't you agree?[231]

*

One thing I got a kick out of that never happened in England was that I didn't date girls my own age. I found out I never had to go out and ask a girl out, they would just be there. I was 16 and was going out with older girls. They dug me because I was a romping "little boy" and that really blew my mind!

It spoiled me a little. Now, I don't like to make dates. I guess girls really hate this, but I don't like to call up on a Wednesday and say "Let's go out at 8 on Sunday," because by 8 on Sunday I might feel terrible. I like to call up a half hour before and say, "Would you like to do this or that." I don't want girls to run after me, but I like to go out when I feel like it.[232]

*

Some of the girls I've dated, and am still dating, have very ordinary jobs and aren't famous or anything at all like that. I date a lawyer's secretary named Eileen, and she's really sweet. And then there's a girl in Hawaii whose name is Perla — I met her when I was there. We went sailing and surfing and did all the things people usually do when they're in Hawaii. Then there's a girl in Texas who lives on a farm. We go riding when I'm down there. I met her through a friend of mine who used to play for The Mets baseball team. In just about every town I travel to there's someone I can call on the phone and take out to dinner. They're people I've met over the last five years or so, since I was in *Oliver!*. In England I used to date my agent's secretary.[233]

*

I was dating a girl at the time [I recorded the pre-Monkees album, David Jones], a girl named Eileen. We [The Monkees] just played the Greek Theater in Los Angeles, and would you believe it, I saw her for the first time in 45 years! She walked in the door, and she just smiles and says, "David." It was Eileen! We hugged. She's married, she's got a daughter, and both her husband and daughter were there, along with her daughter's boyfriend. We spent 45 minutes together. I wasn't in the meet-and-greet that night, I can tell you. I wasn't out there shaking hands with all the people. I just sat in the dressing room with Eileen and her family, because that was a really touching time in my life, you know?[234]

*

I like blondes mainly. I like to be seen out with tall pretty girls and I like to hear people say, "Look at that little guy over there with that girl." It really gives me a giggle... I like to go out with girls who are six feet tall.[235]

*

Maybe you might think it wrong of me but I'm so hung-up at the studio and with my career and everything that I just won't let myself get really involved with *anyone* right now. Whenever I go out, the girls know that it's just for fun, that there's not going to be anything romantic or world-shaking about any of it. I've got girlfriends in most of the cities I've been in and I'll write them a note occasionally, and, of course, if I'm in their town I'll stop by and we'll go out to dinner or do what we enjoy doing, like swimming or horseback riding, and we'll have a lot of fun. Then I'll be off to the next stop on our tour or whatever and we'll have some good memories, nothing more.[236]

*

Then there are the celebrities, like Sally [Field] and Deana [Martin], who are the ones you usually see me with in magazines. The newspapers and the magazines are always trying to get pictures of me with somebody and they usually have a pretty tough time doing it since most of my dates are at home cooking dinner and watching the telly. But when I do go to something like an opening I'll usually go with someone like Sally and Deana because it's the most natural thing to do.

Deana and I have some great times together. I go over to her house and play pool or we have soccer games with Dino and Ricci and Gina and Claudia, or else her mother and father and she and I will watch TV or go out to dinner or something. I really like the Martin family because it's one of the places I can really relax and be myself totally.

Dino will show me his new record, or he and Ricci and I will jam for a while, and everyone will just have a ball. I really think a lot of Deana because she's a true friend.

Sally comes to recording sessions and watches us play or we'll cook dinner and watch TV and it's just a friendly relationship. She's a wonderful person and I hope some day to work with her professionally but there's nothing permanent in the relationship at all.[237]

*

I like to move with different crowds and by dating different girls I get to do this. For instance, at Deana's I meet certain people and at Sally's I meet other people. And the lawyer's secretary introduces me to her friends, and my girlfriend in Hawaii and on and on. I was over at John and Michelle Philips of The Mamas and Papas and I met people like Mia Farrow and Tina Sinatra. It's very interesting to see all those people and see what their scene is. They're all very interesting people to talk to.[238]

*

I've always dated the same type of girls. They don't have to be pretty or anything like that because who wants to sit and talk to a pretty face that can't say anything? I'd rather have a girl who has something on the ball, who doesn't agree with me just because I happen to be David Jones, and who's fun to be with. I also look for neat girls — you know how much I demand neatness and order. But beyond that, they can be most anything — tall, short, skinny, fat — it doesn't matter to me.[239]

Talk About Gratitude

I thought the biggest mistake I ever made was to go into show business. I always wanted to be a jockey. This to me [winning the horse race in 1997] was one of the most exciting times of my life because everything went the way I wanted it to go. It's all about timing.[240]

*

My career was taking me into the racing game, into horse racing, but I did accomplish something by winning that race a couple of years ago, which was something I'd always wanted to do. It wasn't the full force, it wasn't something that I'd imagined I'd be doing — performing all these years later — but I pretty much am doing what I'm supposed to be doing.

There are answers, and questions I need to ask, but I'm sure in the next period, I'll be able to answer a few more than I did the last period.

I'm always looking for the answers, and no fee, it'll be positive as I feel now, and as Micky, Peter and I feel about this tour [2001].

Having a great time. Single. And enjoying life.[241]

*

I was always a bit of a showoff; always in the school play. To me, everything I ever do is absolutely no different than the school play. I really look at it as saying: I'm a lucky son of a gun, and I never ever thought any more of anything I was doing.[242]

*

I am very grateful [to have been in The Monkees], and I'm even more grateful when people tell me they've seen me on the stage in *Oliver!* back in the '60s, or playing Fagin in the '80s and '90s. I'm very proud of all the things I've done in The Monkees, and if I want to say, "It ruined my acting career," that would be true, but then it's up to me to carry on and *change* people's opinions.[243]

*

I'm not as wealthy as some entertainers, but I work hard, and I think the best is yet to come. I know I'm never going to make the Rock and Roll Hall of Fame, but maybe there's something *else* for me in show business. I've been given a talent — however big or little — that has given me many opportunities. I've got to try to use it the best way I can. A lot of people go days without having someone hug them or shake their hand. I get that all the time.[244]

*

I'm looking for answers of my own, a lot of them came through The Monkees experience, and obviously it's empowered and enriched me so much because it's given me an opportunity to communicate with so many different people on different levels.[245]

*

Some people looked down on the series, but look at what I got: two years in front of the camera, learning what to do.[246]

*

Recently I was on a plane, and there were 50 to 100 teenagers from Texas aboard going to Europe for a choir festival. They knew I was on the plane. So I went back from First Class, and they all stood and applauded.

I said, "Stay in your seats, folks, don't rock the plane."

They said, "Davy, come on, sing for us."

So I said, "I'll tell you what, I'll trade you one 'Daydream Believer' for one of yours, but *I'm* singing first."

So I started to sing.

We're 35,000 feet up.

When I finished, they started to sing. These kids were beautiful!

Afterward the pilot came on the loudspeaker and said, "Thank you very much. And thank you, Davy Jones."

And I thought, "I'm such a lucky guy."

In a world of noes I get an awful lot of yeses.[247]

*

There are always drawbacks to any sort of success, whether it's just a personal disappointment. I don't think there were any career drawbacks; I think it was a great thing for me and it's helped me all the way since. I missed out on my late teens, being around and being with my family, my father especially. He did live long enough to see me make a success with The Monkees, so that was: "My son! My son!" You know, as most fathers do.

I missed out with my family and now I'm back in England and I'm seeing more of them. As far as anything else [drawbacks], I don't think so. It was a career that I had chosen, there were ups and downs.

There were more ups than there have been downs, so I'm very fortunate.[248]

*

I was up in Sacramento a couple of months ago and met up with some guys, some veterans that were over in Vietnam in the 60's. I remember shaking their hands as they took off in their planes in the late sixties.

They gave me a t-shirt when I met them again a couple of months ago with pictures of me and them! These were the pictures we took in '68, '67, and they were on their way to Vietnam. And they remembered, and I remembered — I remember the *occasion* not the *faces* obviously because after 25 years, 30 years, faces change, but I was well in touch with that idea.

Unbelievable that I was able to hook up with them again. All came home safely, and that was the name of that tune!

And I was so surprised that The Monkee records were part of their day when they were over there. But The Monkees touched a lot of people, the music touched a lot of people, and I would never have imagined that guys that would be over there in that very unfamiliar surroundings would even consider listening to *our* music, but they *did*!

I'm blessed with many, many, *many* occasions that The Monkees brought good faith and empowerment to a lot of people.[249]

*

I am so blessed. The world is in a horrendous state of economic, social and moral decay at this particular point, and I hope we can just let people forget their troubles for a while.[250]

*

The Monkees touched a lot of people. People have happy memories from that, and not everybody can claim that side of life. I'm vey grateful for what happened with me, I'm very grateful for what happened with my career, and there's more to come.[251]

*

I'm an accessible guy who knows how to ride horses, knows how to fix a roof, and knows how to entertain. In many ways, I've been under-compensated, but in many ways I've been so so lucky.[252]

*

He [Basil Foster] was like a second father to me and I owed him. Without him, I might not be doing what I'm doing today. [*Davy paid the home care fees of his former horse-racing mentor, Basil Foster, in his later years. Basil passed away April 10, 2013 — a year after Davy passed.*][253]

*

Man, [my first ride at Newbury after coming back to racing] was exciting. I also had a few races over hurdles, but I was riding against what I'd call "professional amateurs" — and they used to gang up on me. There were hard men, like Tim Thomson Jones and Jim Wilson, and I once broke my hand in a fall in a two-and-a-half mile hurdle.[254]

*

It was a dream. I'd wanted to ride a winner since I was a kid and I was fortunate enough to realise that dream.[255]

*

Even though acting is a rough life, I love it. I realize that I'll never be able to do most of the things other people take for granted as long as I'm an actor, but it's worth the sacrifice. It's the only job I know of where you can turn sadness into happiness right before your eyes.[256]

*

I wake up in the morning, I go: "I *love* my life. This is *great*." And I go out and I sit on a racehorse and I'm riding around a track, and saying what the heck am I doing up here?

I do everything I want to do.[257]

*

I just want to be positive at this stage. I'm blessed with a variety of [touring] options, and I don't take it all lightly. I got exactly what I asked for [in life], and I'm very happy. I'm trying to be a little bit more aware of my good fortune. I'm learning a lot more in my later years than I did as a youth, when I was more interested in knocking The Grass Roots off the charts.[258]

*

It's kind of strange being a 65-year-old man and people looking at me the way they'd hoped I'd be. That's the aura, the emotion, the feeling that I try to present, on or off the stage: Be positive, be thankful, and be grateful.[259]

Talk About Grief

My mum was ill, on and off, for about seven years. She had chest trouble — which everybody does in Northern England, because of the smoke and smog and harsh weather. She would have to go into the hospital about two months out of every year.

My dad tells me now that the doctor said goodbye to her seven years before she died. She could have gone any time — each year she'd be in an oxygen tent — then she'd recover and come back all spruced up. Then she'd go another few months and collapse again.

Dad says she was waiting for us to grow up. I guess she thought we'd all grown up.[260]

*

A very strange thing happened just before my mother died. A few days before she passed away she cut a poem out of a magazine and she left it in her purse. It's called "Love Still Abides."

> *She has gone beyond the range of sight*
> *Into the glory of the morning light*
> *Out of the reach of sorrow and despair*
> *Safe in the shelter of our father's care*
> *Weep not for her, say not she is dead*
> *For she has gone on a few steps ahead*
> *Faith looks beyond this time of grief and pain*
> *Love still abides and we shall meet again.*

We have it on the piano now at home in a little frame. I think my mother knew she was going to die. She had cut out the poem and put it in her purse.

She wouldn't go to the hospital. She said, "Just let me stay here for a couple of days."

She died that evening.[261]

*

Right after [my mother] died I didn't want to know anybody. It took a while to come out of my shell, but I really believe I've grown stronger as a person. When I was home at Christmas, Dad said that strangely enough, since she died, I've had nothing but good luck.

Everything's been good — I've not stopped working, I've slowly improved my position, and everything has just taken its course. Dad still says now and then, "Your mum's watching over you." And I believe she is.[262]

*

Mum was ill for many years and she had four children in ten years when she wasn't physically fit. I've got three older sisters and my dad wanted a son, but it wasn't in her best interests to have another baby…

I felt guilty, and I've had it said to me many a time, by a wife or sister: "You've never got over the death of your mother," which I haven't.[263]

*

Even though my mother is gone, I have a lot of wonderful memories of times we had together.[264]

*

When my mum died when I was young I felt like it was the end of the world. Then when my dad died not so long ago I realised that I was in a strange position. Right in the middle of a whole lot of people when it came to my work, but right in the middle of nothing when it came to my own life.

I needed a family, I wanted roots. With my sisters being married and having their own lives to lead I felt like some kind of orphan.

I don't think anyone realises just how much family life means to me.[265]

Talk About Growth

Every crisis that comes up you really handle it *yourself*. No matter how you decided what to do, or how much advice someone gives you, in the end it's *you* that makes the decision. That's why I really hate the concept of a psychiatrist. I think that's a joke. You tell him your problems, he's not going to be able to help, you're just getting them off your chest, but that's a cop out. You could do the same thing inside your mind.[266]

*

If you don't have regrets, you're an idiot. There are things that happened in our lives, together and otherwise, that we are not the happiest over. Words stick more than anything, and you've gotta be very careful what you say. I'd rather have a punch on the jaw than someone speak to me in a bad tone.

Years ago, when we did our first tour and I came out of the BBC having just done an interview, there was this young guy there in his twenties and I said, "How you doing, mate?"

And he says, "I'm not your mate!"

And I had to keep walking.[267]

*

To the best I can [I usually try and discover and remove my faults and weaknesses]. The problem is, once you get rid of one fault one week, there's always another to take its place. Otherwise life would be very uneventful and very boring.[268]

Talk About Happiness

Happiness? There's no way *to* happiness, happiness *is* the way.

Change the way you look at things because the things you look at will change.

So if you've been down, and if you've been way, way down… life is like a fish bowl. You get a success, and you get to the top of the mountain. I've been to the top of the mountain, and I've seen what's going on there. And then you slide down a little bit and you handle yourself somewhere on the slope, so that there's always room for dreams. You really don't want to go back down *there* and get your feet wet again. You want to just be comfortable, so stay in that medium of comfort, the comfort zone, find that comfort zone.

Never give up your dreams, never give up your youth.[269]

*

The Monkees were all about laughter. Ask me why The Monkees are not getting together? They don't want to have laughter. They want to be serious. I want to make people laugh.

As a joke, I tell people, "If you remember The Monkees, you're either very young or bloody old!"

Laughter is something people need to *hear* and *feel*.[270]

*

I love to talk to children. I think it's because I was so happy when I was a kid, and I know that they're really happy, and it's good to share all that happiness. You can smile and laugh and talk without all the hang-ups of the adult world. Kids are honest. Maybe that's why they're so out-a-site.[271]

*

But there was a lot of good times [making The Monkees]. More good than bad, you know. It's like the world; there's more good in the world than there is bad, but we always tend to focus on the unhappy moments and the bad things that happen to us. But I think we're getting better. You know, I think we're getting better.[272]

*

Once you get yourself into a happy [place] — there's no *way* to happiness, happiness *is* the way — once you get yourself into a place where you can cope with yourself, then you're able to project that image and that personality and that feeling to the audience, and the audience is the general public.[273]

*

I'm very happy. There's no *way* to happiness, happiness *is* the only way.

It's not a religious thing, I just preach my own way of doing things. Like Fagin said, "Everything *in moderation*, my dear. You know, too much gin is a bad thing for a young girl."[274]

Talk About Honesty

They're *so* groovy, kids are. Adults should be like that — just like kids. They should say what they think and then sort it out afterwards. Otherwise, everything's kept inside.

For example, a kid would take a bite of something and if he didn't like it, he'd say, "I don't like that. I don't want any more." But an adult would probably eat it anyway and then complain about it all the way home, or maybe never go back to that restaurant or those friends' house or something.

I don't mean that adults should be impolite or anything. I just gave this example to explain what I mean when I say that adults should say what they think and then sort it out. Most of the time, adults keep everything inside and get all hung up on their problems, when if they had just stopped and said, "Hey, this shouldn't be that way," everything would have been stopped or straightened out when it began — and not months later.

I think grown-ups can learn a lot from kids about honesty and all.[275]

*

Do you prefer flattery or honest opinion?

I prefer honest flattery.[276]

*

You've *not* got to be afraid to voice your own opinion, as to how you feel. But you've got to be careful when you voice your opinion. It's far easier to be *critical* than it is to be *correct*. So you just listen to an opinion, and if you are going to criticise anything, no matter what it might be, then you do it in a way that is not destructive, but constructive. It's always good to be able to *take* advice.[277]

Talk About Horses

These hands don't *only* hold a microphone; they hold reins and they hold a pitchfork.[278]

*

I'm also very interested in horses, have been all my life. Before I got into show business, I was an apprentice jockey in England in '62, and I was there for a short while.

It's the bug: once you're in, you're in. It's like the Mafia, and I can't let it go.[279]

*

When I left school as a 14 year old, I went straight into the stables as an apprentice jockey. It's been with me all my life. I've got horses now, it's very difficult [competing] these days; you're running against all kinds of thoroughbreds that are really unknown quality. I had one experience at Del Mar a couple years ago, I ran my horse, Indiantown Jones, in the 67th running of the Del Mar Handicap. I was standing on the shed row, and there's this little kid with his dad and mum, and I got some carrots and gave them to him — when you're on the track you're just like everybody else, nobody cares who you are, it's all about the horses. So I gave these carrots to the little kid, he gave them to the horse. His father came over to me before he left the stable, he shook my hand, and when he left, he'd put a twenty in my hand, he says, "Thank you very much."

So, unknown and anonymous, that's what the horses do for me.[280]

*

At the moment, I have six thoroughbreds and I have some other horses: I have a driving horse, I have an Amish carriage, I sometimes ride it round my track at the back of my house.[281]

*

I have a couple of horses, one a beautiful chestnut colt, by Cat Thief, who is just turning two. He's called Bazfoster, named after Basil [Foster]. I'd love to ship him to England, box him up and run him at Newbury or Cheltenham, just so people can remember Basil Foster. That would be so great.[282]

*

We've got another couple coming through; Manchester Boy and C Hoarse (pronounced Sea Horse) and you hope either of them could be something special. I keep dreaming, like all owners.[283]

*

I love this time of year [spring and summer], one of the reasons being, my horses. Once I have finished all my chores, if I haven't ridden in the morning, I can go in the evening.[284]

*

I ride every day when I'm at my own little place in Pennsylvania, or in Carolina. I got horses that are in training and running right now.

I ride thoroughbreds. It's not something you just *do*; it's something that you've got to be very focused about.

I bought a couple of horses at the sales this year in Keenland and hopefully they will turn out to be very, very good animals; you always have these expectations.

I know this is gonna be showing on and off here and there, and time will go by, but I happen to — this very weekend — have a couple of horses running. It's the last steeplechase meeting of the season, and I have two horses, Maternity Leave and Market Neutral, and that's over those big jumps, it's not show jumping it's racing, and it's a great passion for me.

One day I'll be back in England and win the Grand National, so that's the big one.[285]

*

I hope to one day compete in the Grand National, which is a race in England. And more close to home, as I live in Pennsylvania, just a horse ride away, is place called Maryland, and every year they have a race called the Maryland Cup, and I would like to be part of that, either as an owner, jockey, as a trainer, or as all three of those. So I have my sights set on there.[286]

*

It's not about the prize money, it's just about *beating* everybody! I just want to beat *everybody*, you know? Bring 'em on![287]

*

When I sit on that horse, it's not about cameras, it's not about scripts, it's fact. You sit on a thoroughbred racehorse, you feel so powerful and you feel so good about having accomplished this amazing thing. It's like catching a ten pound fish on a two pound line.[288]

*

I'm hands on. I ride them myself, I exercise them myself, and I take them to the track. I do this every day, It's part of my life.[289]

*

I think it's that fatherly thing in a sense; when the kids grow up and move away, then you've got something that's dependent on you.[290]

*

Now I'm going to breed some horses because I feel now, after forty-five years, that I'm qualified, and parenting is a very important part of my life. I've probably got fifteen children. Some have four legs but, you know, hey, what the heck.[291]

*

I have five racehorses in training. I had a nice winner last week at Gulfstream in Florida [2004] — my first win, actually, as a *trainer*. It was a grand slam filly I bought a couple years ago. She paid 40 dollars [laughs]. Her name is T.E. Jones. All my horses are Joneses. People think I own the Kentucky Derby winner [Smarty Jones].[292]

*

What I want more than anything is to *win*. Coming off a stage, I know the audience is going to enjoy some of what I do — being Davy Jones of The Monkees and all that kind of thing. There ain't no Davy Jones or The Monkees when I'm dealing with horses. This is about me, and my horse.[293]

*

Maybe some observe what I'm doing with criticism and think, "Oh, he can't be training horses, he's a Monkee." Or, "He can't ride." Maybe they're waiting for me to fall off or make a mistake. But I can ride a finish as well as anybody, and I'm tough in the jockey room. There are places I go where The Monkees don't come into play.[294]

*

The racing bug is never going to go away. It's like the Mafia. I've still got my first pair of riding breeches, which I showed Basil the other day. He was shocked I'd still got them, but I remember him sending me down Newmarket High Street to buy them like it was yesterday.[295]

*

I was an apprentice jockey in England in the sixties. But it wasn't until a few years ago [February 1, 1996] that I rode my first winner [Digpast] on the track [in the Ontario Amateur Riders Handicap at Lingfield Park in Surrey, England].

I won a mile on the flat.

That was the biggest thrill of my life.[296]

*

New York State
Racing and Wagering Board
JONES, DAVID T.
PO BOX 400
BEAVERTOWN, PA. 17813
OWNER
VALID UNTIL
12/30/2010
License # 1367165
Thoroughbred

Talk About Jokes

The audiences *love* [my jokes], even though they're lousy.[297]

*

My opening line for my show is: "Hello, I'm Davy's dad. Davy will be out here in a minute."

And then I take it from there.

I make fun of the situation, and make fun of myself.[298]

*

Micky, Mike and Peter, they send their love. They're all in the Actor's Home in Hollywood.

I actually went to see them before I left, and I said to Micky [loud and slow]: "Do you know who I am?"

And Peter said: "Ask the nurse; she'll tell you."[299]

*

People like Peter No-one… Peter Noone… (it's spelled no-one where I come from, all right?) he's singing, "Mrs Brown, You've Got A Lovely Walker," these days. Tony Orlando is singing, "Knock Three Times On The Ceiling If You

Hear Me Fall," ABBA is singing, "Denture Queen," Ringo is singing, "I Get A Little Help From Depends," Roberta Flack is singing, "First Time I Ever Forgot Your Face," and Willie Nelson is On The Throne Again. David Cassidy is singing, "I think I love… *Me.*"[300]

*

If you like our show, tell everybody.

If you don't like it, tell them you saw David Cassidy.[301]

*

I told my daughters I was going on The Ellen Show. They said, "What you gonna ask her?"

I said, "I'm gonna say to her, 'Ellen, boxers or briefs?'"

They said, "Do *not* do that, Dad!"

Why not ? She gives so much away all the time. She's giving presents left and right![302]

*

I'm so old [66] this woman came up to me after a performance and said: "I want to give you super sex."

And I said: "In that case, I'll take the soup."[303]

*

Jessica turned to me one day and said: "'Let's run upstairs and make love."

I looked at her.

"At my age," I said, "it's going to have to be one or the other."[304]

*

My love life is life the petrified forest at this point. If I was Indian, I'd be sacred.[305]

*

Did you hear that in India they found a woman with five legs? They said that her knickers must fit her like a glove.[306]

*

I don't practice the tambourine often these days. Sometimes when I'm dusting I take it off the shelf, but dropping it doesn't count, does it?[307]

*

Harry [Secombe] always sticks to the script and doesn't fool around at all. It was the last night [of *Pickwick*], and as Pickwick's valet, Sam Weller, I bring some apples and oranges and some chicken sandwiches every night to the debtors prison, because Mr Pickwick, and all the Pickwickians had been sentenced to the debtors prison. So I'd arrive with this big trunk and I'd carry it down the stairs, and he'd say, "Oh, here comes Sam now."

So, I'd come down with this trunk. I said, "Gov'nor, wait a minute; I've got the apples. And I've got the oranges. I *couldn't* get any bread, so I don't have the chicken sandwiches… But I *do* have… the *chicken*!"

And I opened up this trunk and this chicken that I'd had in my room — for three days in my bath tub in the hotel room — came out and went [imitates clucking chicken]!

Follow that one![308]

*

We played Disneyworld. I like Disneyworld a lot. I fit in pretty good down there. I have a little golf cart, and I go scooting around, and this guy went in front of me, and I said, "Hey, mate! Watch what you're doing, I had the right of way!"

He said, "Okay, okay, okay. Don't be grumpy."

I said, "I'm not grumpy."

He said, "Well, which one are you, then?"[309]

*

I love Japan. We got a standing ovation over there and we didn't even know it![310]

*

I hope you're all doing well, I hope you didn't get too wet. It got a little rainy there for a minute outside, but it doesn't bother me, I can't shrink any more than I have.[311]

*

I'm running short on height. I keep thinking I'm getting shorter, I don't know why. Either that or the floor's getting closer…[312]

*

It's not that we're short, it's that everybody else is so bloody tall! It's not easy looking up people's nostrils all the time.[313]

*

No more short jokes, okay! That's it! They're all going over my head anyway.[314]

*

I loaned Micky Dolenz money for plastic surgery, but the doctor did such a good job I can't find him to get my money back.[315]

*

I love Westerns, you know. I love Westerns. I was so glad when Clint Eastwood finally got an Oscar for a Western. But it would be ridiculous, an *English* Western: "Why did you shoot me, Kevin? Stand back, Graham! All right, John, you're in big trouble now. All right, Sherif, get on that horse and get out of town. Just let me finish me beer and I'll be gone."[316]

*

I like a bit of humour, a bit of hummus.

"Doctor, there seems to be a garbonza bean substance around the patient's heart."

"Oh, well, hummus where the heart is."[317]

*

I was performing a song from *Oliver!* on The Ed Sullivan Show when the Beatles made their American debut.

I remember getting into the lift with Ringo Starr. I was always a cheeky little guy.

He had a cold at the time and I remember saying, "Let me blow your nose for you, I'm closer than you are."

Ringo said, "I know."[318]

*

I'm not afraid of saying anything. I make people cringe sometimes.

One of the worst things I've ever said — and my girlfriend said she had to run off the side of the stage it was so bad — was to this woman who came in late in Vegas the other day.

She was rat-faced (Brit slang for very drunk), so I stopped the song and said, "Where the hell have you been? We've already done three songs and you've missed the best material."

So she says (slurring speech), "I waaassin the baaah. I was in the baaah. I had to get a drink."

I said, "Oh, I'd like a drink as well. Can I suck your tongue?"[319]

*

They had a gay, lesbian, and transvestite night at The Schooners Bar (on the cruise ship). And I walked in and there's this guy-girl, girl-guy, whatever, sitting in the corner, crying away.

And I said, "Excuse me, what's wrong, Miss, Sir, Miss? What's the matter?"

She said, "My partner didn't get on in Aruba. I don't know what to do."

I said, "I tell you what, don't worry. When we get to land we can do some advertising, like they do with missing children, only this time we'll put his picture on cartons on Half N' Half."[320]

*

I love making people laugh and making them happy and the most comforting place for me to be is on stage. It's what I wanted to do when I was a little boy and I still get to do it. I'm on all the time. I just love to entertain.[321]

Talk About Legacy

My last song I wrote said: "Remember me the way you hoped I'd be." And I've seen so much bad behaviour in the business, and it's best that everybody's not thought of the same, so try to set an example.[322]

*

I am about to set up a racing establishment. Around the property I have here [in Pennsylvania], I'm about to put an all-weather race track. I'm about to build stables. I'm about to ship over a couple of my thoroughbreds from England. I'm about to challenge for the Maryland Cup in the next couple of years, as an owner, a trainer, and a rider. This is where I feel I would like to leave a mark. This is why I hold a jockey's license. The show business is another part of my life. My family is a part of my life and everything is all a mixture of enjoyment. I'm 42 years old the end of this month (December) and I'm going to try and cram as much in to it as I can.[323]

*

My Memorabilia Museum is going to complement my situation, my Property Will when I leave, when I'm gone eventually, my epitaph — there's a nice park and a horse training centre, and all those things that one hopes to accomplish before one's final hour.[324]

*

The biggest thing I ever did wasn't selling records or playing to screaming fans. It was being a dad.

If I'm remembered for anything, I hope it's not the hair, or the hit songs — I hope it's that I *loved* deeply and gave people joy.[325]

Talk About Life

I've raced. I have a jockey's license. I ride steeple chase. It's very scary, especially when you're 50 years old next year.

You see, the problem is that when you get older you get a little more brittle, and I've broken fingers and shoulders and ankles and things like that. I'm not saying that it's not because I'm not a good jockey, it's just that one out of ten rides you *do* come off, and you're riding along with ten or twelve guys and these animals weigh over a thousand pounds, and they bang up against each other, they go over the jumps and you never know how they're going to land. Sometimes they dive, sometimes they duck, sometimes they turn, and you're up there with your feet in the irons and you've got to have the balance. It's a massive rush. But there again, if you apply the same technique to life, it's a *balance*.

You've got to *balance* yourself. You've got to know when to push it, and when to ease off.[326]

*

I feel good, you know? If you feel good and you're really interested in whatever it is you're doing, age doesn't matter. Life is very interesting, if you *want* it to be interesting.[327]

*

I t's interesting, I just don't fill my life with any *one* thing. When you've got family and friends, you need to space your time out. And how much time do you have? That's the hardest thing for me to deal with. That somebody else partly has the control of my being here, and not being here. So I try to make it fit.

Every day is the *only* day in the rest of your life. That's the way I feel. And as I say, change the way you look at things and the way you look at things will change.[328]

*

N ot too much of everything. Just a little bit of everything and then feel other people's emotions. That's how you do it, by sharing their occasions. It's not where you are, or what you're doing, it's who you're *with*.[329]

*

I f I had to do it over again, I'd stop a few more times to smell the roses.[330]

*

T he reason I live kind of remote after being in Hollywood all those years, I want to be unknown and anonymous, and I just want to be part of a community, part of a situation. It makes me feel whole, it makes me feel that it's not temporary.[331]

*

You gotta be a little bit tough to do this, you've gotta have a little edge, and I think that's come from me having been in the business for so long, and knowing what it's about. I've never gotten into directing or producing; I kind of put my energy into these animals [horses] the same way as I would into a script that I would write, or a production I would be involved in, so to me, it's my salvation. It gives me stability, it gives me a foundation to work off.

I say to myself: "Oh, well I'm going out to work, I'm going out to make a TV show, I'm going off to play in a concert, because then I'll be able to spend time with my horses."

So that's what we work for — is the *recreation* time, and it's very difficult to "turn off".[332]

*

If I had gone off after The Monkees had finished in 1970 and gone to Hollywood Park, or Santa Anita, and said, "I'm a jockey, I can ride," you don't think I would've got rides? I would've got rides, if only just because of who I was.

So you've got to really pick your moments. It's actually the same thing you've got to do on a horse, really.

The best horse is not always the horse that wins the race: it's the jockey that makes the least mistakes.

And I don't think I've made too many mistakes so far, because I haven't been overplayed. Although I may overplay *myself* a bit…[333]

*

I haven't really done a lot of European travel, and just because of the occasion I wouldn't mind going to Rome and to Dusseldorf and go to some of those historic cities that have been in the history books as "places to visit". But it doesn't matter; you know the secret to life? It's not where you are or what you're doing, it's who you're with. That is the secret. So [right *here*] is the favourite place I want to be. Not everybody's where they want to be, not everybody's doing what they want to do, but fortunately it's worked out for me and I got exactly what I asked for.[334]

*

I've been involved with horses all my life. It's my escape from what I do. It gives me something else. I've just written a song called, "I Don't Want to Be Davy Jones Anymore," and I'm like, [singing] "and I don't want to be *me* anymore…"

I go places, and sometimes it's overwhelming. When people see me they say, "Hey, you look so great. I can't believe you look just like you did."

I'm like, Yeah, right. I'm dragging my ass in the morning like you are when you're getting out of bed.[335]

*

It's all depending on the *quality* of life.

I'm sitting here in a beautiful suite at the Radison, and it's my way of life, and I make comfort for myself, and I have my possessions around me, and my pictures of my children, and I just *enjoy* what I'm doing.

I have homes in Pennsylvania, as well as California, and Florida, so I'm very lucky, but I've been doing this for 40 years plus, way before The Monkees, so I should be able to afford some luxuries.

And that's why I do it, to sustain my lifestyle. If you have pleasures then you can't put a price on them.

My price is having to go on the road for a number of months of the year in order to accommodate my expenses.

Basically, that's it.[336]

*

Isn't it too bad that adults can't retain the best qualities of children? They look at each day like it's a new adventure — they wake up every morning with a clear head. The things that bothered them the day before are gone after a good night's sleep.

That's the way to be: grown up, but in some ways, still like a kid.[337]

*

You've just got to find your niche in life. You take yourself seriously when it comes to being on time and performing for a certain amount of time. But the rest of it is acting; it's performing.[338]

*

Some tips I'm gonna give you as far as [cruise ships], okay? The cabins are really small. Every time you come out you feel like you're being born again.

Tips for what you do in the shower, because that's small, too: you just soap the walls and spin.

It's the only place I know you can sit on the toilet and brush your teeth at the same time. Do not sit and flush, whatever you do. There's a suction that goes on there. I sat down, I was Catholic, when I got up I was Jewish![339]

*

I've always been involved in racehorses and I rode my first winner a couple of years ago to commemorate my fiftieth birthday. My daughters bought me a horse, went to the track in England and, lo and behold, won by six lengths, a mile on the flat! That was another dream come true, so all my dreams are coming true. I'm continually performing and writing. I have a new book called *Daydream Believin'*, a lot of things on the burner.[340]

*

Being a financier, or whatever it might be, the idea is not what you've *got*, it's what people *think* you've got; it's not what you've *done*, it's what people *think* you've done; so whatever it is, whatever has happened in your life, personal things are all to do with yourself and the people around you.

Accept it or don't accept it.

Deal with it as it comes. Deal with it as it comes.[341]

*

Life is so precious and you got to live it to the fullest and just be considerate to other people.[342]

*

Talk About Marriage

I want very much to have a good marriage someday, complete with a wonderful family, and a cute little house, and the whole bit. But that's going to have to wait for later because now my career is the most important thing in my life. After my career gets settled and I get really established permanently, then I'll begin to think about starting that home and family I want so much.[343]

*

I can't help but laugh when magazines say that in the near future I'll be marrying one or another of the girls I date. With all the girls I date now, and with all the ones I'm constantly meeting, how could I possibly choose one above all the others to spend the rest of my life with? It's just too unrealistic right now. Someday, after I've dated many, many girls (including a lot that I haven't even met yet!) I'm going to find someone that I do want to spend the rest of my life with, but it's going to take a long time and a lot of dating first! But when I do choose to marry, it's going to be the sort of marriage that you read about in fairy tales — the "till death do us part" kind, complete with a home and family to make everything just perfect.[344]

*

I won't care if my wife has a career; she can do whatever she wants as long as she's home when I'm home. I don't care about her making dinner as long as there's something to snack on in the ice box. You know yourself if you have someone staying over for a couple of days that everything gets out of place. I like to be able to go to the ice box and if I want a cream soda, I can have a cream soda. If I want some cheese, I know it's there. But when someone stays with you, you put the cheese there — the Dutch cheese you really dig — but when you want some, it may be gone.

I think I'll be very easy to live with for this reason. But my wife will have to be understanding, too. Suppose I told her in the morning I would be home at seven o'clock, and at five to seven I called up and said, "Darling, I can't make it home because I have to record." She'll have to understand. But I'll be understanding of her, too.[345]

*

When I find the girl I want to marry, I'll get married! I don't care if she's short or tall, thin or fat—I don't mind that. I like girls to be attractive — not necessarily pretty or beautiful — but they can be attractive to talk to. I know a lot of girls that aren't very attractive looking, but they have great minds.[346]

*

I remember the first concert. It was in Hawaii. We were at Miss Teenage America. There was three thousand screaming kids, a built-in audience. It was amazing. Actually, I met my wife there, Linda, my first wife. I loved Hawaii. I'd been there a couple of times before.[347]

*

It wasn't that my marriage [to Linda] had ended; it was that I had failed. I'd never imagined *not* being married forever. That was the plan, and the plan didn't work out. I was never promiscuous and I didn't have a bevy of girlfriends, but after the divorce I went a bit crazy and had a couple of affairs. It was anger about the divorce, and feeling a failure, a sense of abandonment.[348]

*

The [first two marriages] didn't work because I was looking for something and wanting to go somewhere. I just didn't know where it was I wanted to go. When you're an entertainer and become successful, you suddenly become better looking, more articulate, even taller in some cases! But it's just not true and it takes a while to understand that.[349]

*

It's been difficult for me to sleep on my own — I need to feel an arm, that comfort, next to me.[350]

*

When I saw [Jessica], I thought: "Wow, she's hot!" But she was 28.

Then she looked me up on the computer and went: "Oh my God, he's 60!"

I liked her, but nothing happened. So I bought her a dress and when she put it on, it fitted perfectly. Her family came to the show and she invited me to have dinner with them afterwards. They were probably thinking: "What's this old guy doing here?" I'm older than her parents, for goodness sake!

But after six weeks, we finally got together. We've been together ever since.[351]

*

It was December 18, 2006. [Jessica and I] were going to rehearse for *Cinderella*, a production we were both in. I saw this little girl walk in with her mother, and I thought the mother was playing Cinderella. Turned out the little girl was Jessica and she was playing Cinderella. She looked like she was 15 years-old. She didn't know who I was.

After that first rehearsal, I was thinking about Jess. I called up the producers to find out more about her. They told me she was 28 years-old, and I thought, "Hmm, that's okay, then! I'm not as much of a pervert as I thought I was!"

I went to a shop in the mall and bought her a dress and a purse, since her birthday had passed. The next day, I saw her in the show's parking lot. I walked past her three times, because I just wanted to leave the gift in her dressing room. I gave it to her, and she tried it on later and said, "It fits!" [like Cinderella's shoe.]

We've discussed things, and spoken about the relationships we've both had. Jessica is an old soul. She has traveled the world and is extremely educated. When it comes down to "Jessie and David", we bring the good things into our relationship, and we try to avoid and side-step the things that have made us unhappy before. So you try to be more civil. You wake up every morning and you say, "Good morning, Mrs. Jones."

[*Jessica: "Hello, Mr. Jones."*]

And we go on from there.

At least that's a good start. Sure, we get huffy with each other, but it's not like we take it anywhere else.[352]

*

Of course [there's no physical abuse towards me], the arguments are all verbal. But we do know how to niggle each other. I get niggled by the fact she doesn't pick up the paper in the morning or watch the six o'clock news, but then she gets annoyed when I stir my tea and leave the spoon on the counter. Not that I'm comparing my wives, but Jessica's hugely talented — an amazing actress and dancer — and she's got a psychology degree, which she probably needs with me.[353]

*

One time, [Jessica and I] were listening to the radio, and Jess said, "I love this singer! Who is this?" and it was Mel Torme. She wanted to meet him.

I said, "He's been dead for ten years."

[*Interviewer: So you like the old stuff, Jessica?*]

Hence, that's why I'm here.[354]

*

My wife — a fabulous dancer, great actress, beautiful woman — she's the backbone of what's going on for my life right now, and she's somebody that hopefully will be able to direct me, and help me in the years to come.[355]

*

It's like: "What's Dad going to get next — a Ferrari?"

But when two people are attracted to each other there's nothing you can do.

My eldest daughter said: "Dad, whatever makes you happy is what we want for you and everything else is by the by."[356]

Talk About Michael Nesmith

Mike Nesmith walked in for his audition, and he had a bag of laundry over his shoulder. He had his pants tucked into his boots, which came up to about his knees. He had his wool hat on even though it was the middle of summer.

I thought, "This guy's just come out of the mountains! What's going on here?"

So he came in and said, "I don't have much time. How long is this gonna take?"

And I thought, "Oh, we got a rare one here."

He was on Colpix Records; that's why he was brought in. He never sat down; he just stood there. He was going to do his laundry.[357]

*

Mike really cracked me up when he came in. He walked in with his wool hat, blue jeans and a western shirt, and a laundry bag with his laundry in it — he was afraid to leave it in his car. When Lester (Sill) asked him if he had any pictures, he said yes. And he was told to go home and get them and come back. He was back in 15 minutes — and he was still hanging onto the laundry bag! He just broke me up.[358]

*

Actually, Mike Nesmith was signed to Colpix Records, the same record company I was signed to — Michael Blessing — so they knew about him. I remember him walking into the audition. I'm sitting there with Lester Sill and with the Executive Producer, and he walks in with his pants tucked into his high boots up to his knees, and he had a cowboy shirt on, and he had his laundry over his shoulder, and he said, [adopts southern drawl] "How long is this gonna take?"

And I went, "Wow, man, we don't want this guy!"

I never ever thought that he was gonna be part of the Monkees, but I think that he filled a gap and a place in the show that we wanted that sort of straight face…[359]

*

I remember when I first moved into Hollywood in '65 and the pilot was taking place and I was staying in a hotel or something, and the producers suggested I go stay with Mike, and rent a room from him or whatever. And I remember I thought it was very strange, we'd sit in there and all of a sudden he'd disappear, and he'd go to bed without saying goodnight; I thought that was kind of weird.[360]

*

I stayed with Mike, too, for a while, in between the pilot and the airing of the first episode in September '66. I stayed with Mike and his wife Phyllis and little Christian in his house up on Sunset Plaza Drive in Hollywood.[361]

*

A nd Mike used to invite us all up to dinner. Phyllis would cook — and she'd cook *big*. If Mike had 10 dollars, he'd go out and buy 10 dollars worth of food.

He'd have five or six people and they'd have the best steak, the best vegetables and a wonderful dessert. Phyllis would manage to make it on that. And then they'd eat canned food for the rest of the week. That's the type of guy Mike is. He'd spend his last dollar on somebody.

He just bought his brother-in-law a $3,000 car, and he bought his best friend a Buick Riviera. It's really great.[362]

*

P hyllis Nesmith. She was a wonderful lady. Great girl. I remember little Christian, Mike's son. Mike was a Christian Scientist and his wife, too, and Christian was very, very sick. He had yellow jaundice or something. I snuck him to the doctor's.

Oh! I shouldn't have said that.[363]

*

I love to play with children because they laugh and smile and they're so happy. I like to just fool around. Like when I go to Mike's house, I fight with Christian, wrestle with him and get on top of him and hold his hands down and things like that. He puts his feet on my chest and flips me over and all that kind of stuff and he always starts laughing. Kids like to fight and wrestle — I always do with Christian. I think he expects it. He always comes running to me whenever I walk in the door.[364]

*

Mike Nesmith used to learn a word a day. He had a dictionary. A word a day, and he'd try to use it as often as he could throughout the day.[365]

*

Mike was a sophisticated person and learned a new word every day, so we'd look it up in the dictionary and start using it on him just to piss him off.[366]

*

Mike used to come in with a new word every day, so that word would be used all the time. And it was something you couldn't spell or even repeat.[367]

*

It would have been nice if Mike had been a little bit more vocal, which he never really was. It was all insular. He was always in his own little room.[368]

*

And Mike Nesmith, he certainly had a lot of authority and a lot of leadership; he was supposed to be the leader of the band really. He was the one that figured everything.[369]

*

I remember Christmas time, I bought all the guys a little color TV. Not too many color TVs around in those days.

I went over to Gene Ashman's house for dinner one night. I said, "That's a nice TV. I bought the guys one like that."

He said, "Oh, Mike gave me that."[370]

*

He was never, ever part of that little team. At our first Christmas when we'd be filming, I bought them all a portable, color TV for their dressing room. I liked to give presents — it was a fun thing to do. They all thanked me very much. Then leaving the studio that night, and there's our makeup man with a TV under his arm, the one I'd given to Mike. He gave it to the makeup man! Kind of weird. It was a nice gesture on his part, but you know…[371]

*

You know, he never wanted to be part of what was going on. It was such a sad shame because there could have been a hundred guys out there that would have probably just eaten it up, instead of fighting the feeling, but I guess there were qualities that he brought to the band, and obviously the public were very endearing to him, you know. He had his style, his image.[372]

*

It was tough to convince Mike. It was sort of like philosophy, in a sense that sometimes when you have everything, you just get confused as to what is valuable and what is worthy. How worthy you are of it. And I think maybe it comes from childhood. Michael was a loner for the most part. He was always different. He was always sort of out there with another idea. He was from, I think, San Antonio, Texas, so you know, a musician with long hair in San Antonio, I mean, wow, in the sixties — he must have been going through, "Are you a boy or a girl, boy?" Or whatever it was. Not meaning to be prejudice, but it is quite how it was in those days, you know.[373]

*

Mike Nesmith was terribly unhappy about the music, and that became the main focus of our problems, really, and we shouldn't have really had any problems at this point.

We should have been just doing a TV show and making records and touring and doing interviews and being chased by the fans.[374]

*

And Mike was *always* the guy out there stirring the ladle. When things were going good, *that's* when he stirred harder, and I had no idea why. We didn't know much about him.[375]

*

I was listening to some Mike Nesmith songs the other day and, just because he isn't going to join us, doesn't mean we can't include some of his material. He was so absolutely prolific.[376]

*

Mike was busy writing the B-sides to the singles. Of course, the B-side makes as much money as the A-side and so while my first cheque for record royalties in 1967 was $240,000, his must have been about $5 million. No wonder he doesn't show up for these reunions. I wouldn't either!'[377]

*

I was always wondering why [Mike] drove an Eldorado convertible, and I had a Volkswagen. Because he was a song writer and he had each of the B Sides on our singles.

(The Monkees had one or two *singles*. And then we had some *threesomes* as well!)[378]

*

But something else for you to watch out for is Mike's LP "Wichita Train Whistle", because it's real groovy. I understand it will be released in Britain some time around now, on the Dot label. Don't expect any Monkee business from it, though, because this is Mike veering off in a completely different direction. He got a real kick out of conducting those guys, especially as some of them are top names in jazz. He wondered how they'd take to a pop star conducting them but, though he won't say so himself, it's true that they very soon developed a great respect for him. The whole operation helped Mike relax... you know what they say, a change is as good as a rest, and we haven't had much resting time in the last couple of years or so.[379]

*

Mike Nesmith was responsible for a lot of what's happening in country music today. He was the first one to get into a lot of country rock. He wrote great songs, had hits on his own — wrote Linda Ronstadt's first hit, "Different Drum". He just didn't want to do certain things. He didn't want to have to look back at this time, 40 years later, seeing himself being stupid.[380]

*

He was very authoritative in many, many ways, you know. He got hold of the boys a couple of times. He never got hold of me… because he couldn't *catch* me! Ha ha.[381]

*

It was kind of strange, there was always a bit of tension there with Mike because he'd never really *joined* the band, you know? We performed, and it was great on the TV, and he had his role to play — pretty much who he was. Very seperate. Very aloof. Very distant. Never shared ideas. Never shared stories. Never elaborated on the weekend's activities.[382]

*

Mike never really came into that [playing softball together] scene, he wasn't an athlete, and we never got that side of Michael, you know, casual side. We worked together as a team.[383]

*

Mike was always a little of stand-offish.[384]

*

I would definitely have to say that Michael had the biggest breasts. And if you want to know what they really looked like you just have to check out his head, because that's how big his breasts were.[385]

*

The hat came *with* the hair. It was all one piece.[386]

*

Well, he was well-bald, wasn't he! That hat came with the hair actually.[387]

*

He's cheap. Very cheap. He wakes up in the morning and he looks underneath the bed to see if he's lost any sleep, this is a cheap man.[388]

*

He told us to tell everybody that he doesn't like to tour so just get over it![389]

*

He's not an entertainer in the sense that Micky, Peter and I are. He has his back to the audience half the time. [He's] a brilliant businessman [but] as a person, I haven't got time for him. He's very aloof and separate.[390]

*

He has a different idea. He's going into his later years as a philosopher, as a person of great sort of intelligence. And not that we don't have intelligence, it's just that we are the entertainers — Mickey, Peter and myself. He was more the father of the band, you know, and now he's more sit back and watch his sons go out there and do it again.[391]

Talk About Micky Dolenz

You know this TV show that Micky was in, *Circus Boy*. It actually never really came up that often during the press or the publicity promotions throughout The Monkees thing. It never really came as a question that was asked by the press or other people. Sort of baffled me, really, because I was a big fan of Micky's when I was a little boy![392]

*

I used to watch Micky when I was a little boy, I enjoyed his show, *Circus Boy*, it was one of my favourites.[393]

*

Micky was used to being on the set. Everyone knew him anyway, you know. All of a sudden, he was being remembered ten years later, after the show had finished, and the same people were at the studio.[394]

*

I actually lived with Micky. We had a house during the period in between this pilot and the time we went on the air and started shooting six months later. It was a very tough time, a very tough time.[395]

*

icky Dolenz and I were driving down Benedict Canyon in 1966, before the Monkees show ever came on the air, and we'd already made the pilot and we weren't sure what was going on.

And we were living together — we weren't a couple or anything like that, we were not "doing it" or nothing like that — we were down Benedict Canyon (in Micky Dolenz's '65 green Fastback Ford Mustang, I might add. Hello!) And all of a sudden, on the radio, KHJ played a song…

And that was it![396]

*

e were in London, Micky and I, and I took him for a walk around this particular area, kind of trendy area, with all these like trendy shops, and we got chased and went into a pub, and got chased out of there, and finally headed to the hotel. Back door wouldn't open. Ran to the front. Two big glass doors. And I can honestly tell you, we actually *pulled* the doors off! This was like with *fear* of so many people on our tails, chasing us. It was a game, but it was not always as comfortable as you'd want it to be.[397]

*

I'm not like a showbiz kind of guy that's at all about the parties, and the red carpets, and this, that, and the other. Micky is into that. Micky is a corporate entertainer. He wants to be at these places.[398]

*

Micky and I had a scuffle once in a while, you know, only because you spend so much time with somebody and boys will be boys.[399]

*

Micky Dolenz, he's, you know, he's a stabber. He takes the fork and stabs at the plate. There's bits of china going all over the place usually.[400]

*

There's nothing like smashing a couple of eggs over a friend's head, and then some flour and a bit of rice pudding, you know. Food fights are great in the right place. Every time Micky has a meal, he has a food fight.[401]

*

Micky Dolenz was busy at that time [after The Monkees] trying to develop his own career as a director; he's a fabulous director, got great ideas, and he knows the camera, he's been in the business all his life, so he should know the camera.[402]

*

We played Wembley Stadium and we played big arenas all around Europe and England and Australia and Canada — and I can honestly say, for not having been a drummer at the time, he certainly can pound it out now. Great, great, great, basic, in your face, drummer.[403]

*

I couldn't imagine sharing a stage anymore [2009] with Micky Dolenz, who doesn't want to play the drums, and wants to play the guitar at the front of the stage.[404]

*

Micky and I "pal"ed out more than anything. As we do now, we're still good friends and enjoy each other's company.[405]

*

I admire Micky. I admire Micky very, very much. I think he's a great actor. He's obviously a great singer. He's probably one of the best voices in pop, always has been. He can sing all night and just keep going and going and going, and he's got a great range.[406]

Talk About Money

My family was poor. It didn't bother me, though, because everyone for miles around us was poor, too. We had a small house with nice furniture, but we never had any money in the bank.[407]

*

Sometimes there would be Sunday School picnics and I would get one shilling and sixpence (that's about 25 cents) spending money each week — a shilling from my father and sixpence from my mother. What I would do is save my money all week long and on Sunday I'd buy my mother her favorite candy — Blue Lady Chocolates — and they cost tenpence. That left me with eightpence to spend. So with that, I'd buy a sixpence drink and a two penny candy bar, and I'd make that last all day.[408]

*

Over [in America] you can get into big business, and you can see big business in action. Here [in England] you can't because if you're born middle class that's where you — nine times out of ten — you're going to end up.[409]

*

I n England, you really haven't got much opportunity [to make money]. All my mates, they're earning this three pound, four pound a week, and they've got nothing! They can't save up and get out get out because you need a lot of money to travel to America — to get *shot* or whatever you want to do there![410]

*

I think there's too many people, there's too much class distinction in this country [England]. We still have the lower class, the middle class, and the upper class, and we've got the other people that are running the country and telling us what to do — the people that have already got the money — so my dad can never be a millionaire, and the middle class people can never make any more money than they're making, unless they go out and have a couple of bob on the horses, and that's taxed anyway now. There's no opportunity, unless you've got some talent in show business, or you're gonna invent something, you've got no chance in this country.

Not like America. They say: "You can become a millionaire overnight!" Well, you *can* because that's the kind of country it is — but you've got to take the other thing too, with this *bang bang* business [RFK assassination].[411]

*

I needed some money, so Bert [*The Monkees* producer] gave me $15,000, put a bunch of papers in front of me and said, "Just sign here, Davy."

Unknown to me at the time, that meant a flat $450 a week, including merchandising and everything, and all sorts of — *you can't talk to these people; you can't do this or appear there without our consent* — clauses. All this stuff that I didn't read inside a twenty-five page contract. All I had in mind was home, sisters, Dad. I used the money to get back to Manchester for Christmas, buy a car for my sisters, and a house for my dad.[412]

*

We made very little from the TV series, but we each collected record royalties of over a million dollars before it was all over.

I remember that Micky didn't think our first LP would sell at all and Don Kirshner said to him, "Okay, if you feel that way, I'll give you $50,000 for your royalty payments."

None of us knew that we would do so well out of the things on the side.[413]

*

It was just one good fun time. We had money in our pockets, we were driving our new cars, and it wasn't about dollars and cents at the end of the day.[414]

*

I didn't know about royalties. In fact, we were in the studio one day and these guys are all jamming and we made up a song as we're talking ["No Time"].

Then we came out the studio and we go into the booth and the engineer says, "Hey man, that was cool. What was that?"

And we said, "What did we do? We don't remember what we did."

He said, "It sounds great, this. We ought to do something with this."

We said, "You can have it."

We gave him the publishing on the song and everything. He bought a friggin' house in the Valley for $75,000 with his royalties statement! We weren't making that kind of money! We were making four hundred dollars a week for getting up at that time in the morning and going into the studios.

But we didn't care. We had a TV show, we were acting, and we became friends.[415]

*

Out of the first year, we each made a million dollars each from those small percentages (1 1/4%) and from the salaries we made. In the second year, we made more. But the money was not invested wisely. I was underpaid from Screen Gems, but they still paid me a million dollars. It was when I got it back to where I was, that strangers who came into my life ripped me off.

My dad used to say: "Spend a third, and put a third in the bank. A third is going to taxes; a third is going to your savings; and a third you can spend."

But I never did that. I let other people handle my money. Bad investments were supposedly made. I got ripped off. It took me most of the early 70's, from 1970 to 1975, to pay off the taxes I owed on the money I made from The Monkees. And it wasn't until 1976, when I went out with Dolenz, Jones, Boyce, and Hart that I was free and clear of any financial obligations.[416]

*

The money — they did it very well. And now I come to think about it, I think, "God they really *did* me. They really twisted me inside out."

But I was doing nothing when they got hold of me, and they paid me $450 a week for the first year on the TV show. The second year, it went up to $750 a week. And the guy on the next set that had just been discovered, who had done nothing before, was making $3,000 a week!

But they played it right. I'm glad they did it that way; I think of all the money that I could have made early on, but I'm glad they did it that way because we would have got too cocky in the beginning, you see. They didn't give us money for a year and a half, I swear to you, for a year and a half I'd borrow, or we'd go over to Mike's, and we'd switch, he'd have a meal at my house… They never laid any money on us. They kept us away from that until we were established, and we knew where we wanted to go. They kept all the money away, and all the glamour. I still had the same suit after a year and a half, I had the same car, I swear to you. They handled it right. They knew what they were going to do in the beginning, and they played it the same way all the way along the line.

Now it's a little different, we're in a lawsuit with them because we figure nobody can be called "The Monkees" and we want to own the name because they're going a little commercial with bubble gum and pens and that's not good.[417]

*

We made $400 a week for doing *The Monkees.* [In the second year] $750 a week. We had no merchandise [royalties]. In fact, in our last tour in '69 to Australia, there was a $60,000 *fee* paid for two concerts. We went to Japan for $90,000, and when we came back they sent us a bill (because we were breaking the whole thing up at that time) they sent us a bill for $14,000 each, deficit, because the pencils, the phone calls, the this, the that, the other, and they piled it all in, and before they broke the whole thing up, they sent us a bill!

Not saying we didn't get money from royalties — we had 5% between the four of us, so that's one-and-a-quarter percent each. I remember my first check was for a quarter of a million dollars and that was for one-and-a-quarter percent, so how much money was being made by other people? It baffles me to think. We have renegotiated over the years. I do make $15,000, $20,000 a year from that kind of stuff, but hey, I still have to work.

But it's opened so many doors, and gotten so many benefits from being a part of that show. So that $400 doesn't mean nothing because *this* kind of love and affection that I've gotten from being "Davy Jones from The Monkees", it's crazy. You don't believe what my life's like.[418]

*

Donny Kirshner did hand us all a check for $240,000, our first royalty check, and the money came in after that.

The problem was, other people came aboard at the time. I had a guy come around who stole money from me and left me penniless in the late '60's, early '70's, and I still had to pay the tax on the money! It took years to recover from that. A $50,000 gig on *The Tom Jones Show* helped, and *The Tennessee Ernie Ford Thanksgiving Day Special* helped, but it wasn't gonna recover me from the hundreds of thousands of dollars that just walked away from me. The lawyer's not gonna work for you on contingency if you say, "He stole it and I don't have it."

It was just taken out of my account: power of attorney, bank accounts. It happens to everybody. Everybody's gone through that.

My father said, "You learn by your mistakes, son."

No, you don't *have* to learn from your mistakes. You just have to either carry a big stick, or have people around you. You need a good, legitimate firm, somebody that's not unknown around the world — although that doesn't always work for you either, after what we see in the stock market, and all that's going on lately.

But you don't need someone who believes in you and your talent and wants to go with you all the way and be your buddy. You need a legitimate, bonded lawyer or company. We've all seen it happen with different court cases where the lawyers made a difference. They come up with one little word or phrase that they pinpoint as being negative, and all of a sudden we have a mistrial.

I've had a few mistrials in my life. But I have a beautiful home in Santa Barbara at the polo fields. I have a beautiful house in Pennsylvania. I was divorced a number of years ago, and I had a beautiful mansion estate in England that I handed over to my wife.

So all those years went by, and The Monkees opened the door for me to be able to do a commercial in Macon, that's showing even now, and voice-overs; being the voice in a doll for Mattel. This came after all The Monkee stuff.

The Monkees gave me $450 a week the first year and $750 a week the second year. We probably make about $20,000 a year in royalties on The Monkees, which, when you think that they sold 70 million records, is not a lot by today's standards, but it's a lot more than a lot of people take home for a year's work.

So I can't sustain these homes that I have — and my racehorses, my car, my horse trailer, all those things — by sitting around and thinking, "Oh, I've been hard done by." I work because I want to, and because I want to sustain the lifestyle I have.

I was in Vegas on the 27th of December, I've done symphonies last year; this year I'll be doing them as well. There's so many different avenues for me to go down, and it's only because I'm a professional. I've been in this all my life, since I was 11 years old. I was 63 on Dec. 30.

I need underwear and socks. That's all I care about.[419]

*

Supposedly they made $38 million in merchandising in two years, and we were supposed to share five per cent. I'm suing them now because we didn't get it.[420]

*

I'm not mad anymore because last year we made a lot of money. This year (1987) we made a lot of money. I was mad at Screen Gems, but I'm not mad at them anymore. I'll be mad at them again when I have the time to sue their asses. But I'm not mad at them until that particular time happens. I am glad I was able to put it down in the book [*They Made a Monkee Out of Me*], so people know. The thing is, the reader doesn't want to hear about bad times. They don't want to hear about my million dollars in the bank. They want to know I'm doing good, the fans do. My existence is oh, so very positive. I don't think I've got any negative things running through my life at this point, and Screen Gems is certainly not going to be upsetting me.[421]

*

Well, you see, it's very tricky [the money from Rhino Records re-issues.] Columbia licenses it to Arista. Arista Records does another licensing deal with Rhino Records. And then Arista will do another deal with, say, Silver Bullet Records. Now, somewhere at the bottom of the contract it says something like, in case they put it in a record club, or other avenues of exposure, the royalty rate will drop down. We were on 1 1/4% each. The first check I ever got was for $240,000. So that was 1 1/4% of the first album. That's 5% between us. Where did the other 95% go? How much was it? Who got it? That's what I would like to know. And so by the time it's gone from Columbia to Arista, Arista licenses it to Rhino, and then Rhino licenses it to Silver Bullet, I mean, my 1 1/4% looks like tea money, you know? Although The Monkees had nine albums on the charts last year, re-issues, we made very little money from it.[422]

*

I never looked at it as being dollars and cents at the end of the day. Obviously I have expenses and I like to make money to be able to treat myself.

My first love has always been horses: I'm a jockey; I've a jockey's license; I've a racing stable in England that trained the first Grand National winner back in 1867; I've always dreamt of winning the big race — the Grand National, or the Maryland Cup, or I understand they have jump races also in Tennessee — that's my business, I train jumping racehorses, and that's always been my love.

It's very nice to do the art for art's sake, but there are a lot of people that are out there that have a lot of good touches and they're lucky, and if they're sensible they will have good representation and they will have people supporting them to be able to help them follow through, help them save a little bit.[423]

*

Absolutely no residuals [in 1988]. *The Monkees* show is shown all over the world, and it was shown all over America throughout the years — we don't get residuals. This is a very, very big problem I have with them, being able to explain to myself why I have a union, Screen Actors Guild, or AFTRA, or a union like that, they have gotten a deal with the companies where they pay first, second, third, or fourth reruns, and then they don't pay any more, but they still show the TV show.[424]

*

I never got paid one penny for the *Head* movie, and it's not something that I wouldn't endorse, it's just something that I didn't benefit from in any way, professionally, personally, or financially. I mean, good luck to it, whatever happens with it is fine with me. We got $1,000 each for doing that movie.

It doesn't always have to be dollars and cents at the end of the day. It can be something that people enjoy, people remember, and happy memories.[425]

*

I will be working, and there's only one thing I want is to make people happy and perform. You perform for the money also, let's not get away from that, everybody's in it for that green stuff.[426]

*

In the end, it's not about dollars and cents. We recently came back from The Boys and Girls Club of Florida. It's about a give-back mentality. We've been so blessed, so we like to do stuff like that all the time.[427]

*

It's not a case of dollars and cents. It's a case of satisfying yourself. I don't have anything to prove. The Monkees proved it for me.[428]

*

My advice financially would be spend a third, save a third, invest a third. Because you need that to take care of all those things that you want — that new guitar or that new piano or that new piece of machinery that's revolutionising your recording career. But I don't think you've got to go into it thinking, "This is going to make me a millionaire." If it does, you're lucky, but don't think that you're only doing it for the money, because art doesn't sort of take that form.[429]

*

13 August 1966

PAY TO THE ORDER OF Sherman Oaks Vetrinary $ 25.00

Twenty Five and 00/00 DOLLARS

LOWER-SUNSET BRANCH
6101 Sunset Blvd., Hollywood 28, California

Bank of America
NATIONAL TRUST AND SAVINGS ASSOCIATION

David Jones

16-321
1223

Talk About The Monkees

There was a song in *Pickwick* in which I sang, "I'm as clever as a monkey in a banyan tree." I thought it would be a good idea to form a group called The Monkeys. I'd sing songs with a monkey on my shoulder, just like one of those guys at a barrel-organ. Then Screen Gems came up with an idea for a show in which I'd have two parts, playing cousins. It was going to be called The Monkeys but the idea became *The Patty Duke Show*.[430]

*

I had already signed to Columbia Screen Gems and gone and looked at *Wackiest Ship in the Army*, *Hogan's Heroes*, and a bunch of other stuff. I'd done *Farmer's Daughter* and *Bewitched* and a bunch of programmes, so they were just waiting to find these guys, you know what I mean?[431]

*

They placed me in [*The Monkees*] as a contract player, so I was already in the mix before the auditions were held. In fact, I was at a lot of the auditions. I was at Mike Nesmith's audition, with my manager at the time who became the executive producer, Ward Sylvester. And so I was quite in tune with what was going on. We actually went to see all kinds of bands like Arthur Lee and Love. The bass player in the band was good; we thought that he'd be good, they looked at The Loving Spoonful being a band they could use. Stephen Stills was in consideration.

So there's many different artists, and I, as I say, was at the beginning because of my contract playing with Columbia.[432]

*

They had this idea about at television show about a rock 'n roll group that was trying to make it in the rock n' roll scene. And it may be not known that during that time they were putting *The Monkees* show together, there were other artists trying to do the same kind of idea. People like the Beach Boys and Jan and Dean, they were making pilots also, but The Monkees show was the one that was accepted. Columbia Pictures decided upon this one show, this format, and then they needed four lads for the roles. I was under contract, so I had the part, they placed me in it, and we found the three other boys. They auditioned about 500 lads from England and America and all around the world, and finally they got it down to the four lads from twelve to eight to six and then finally — you, you and you![433]

*

Let me just try and sum it up briefly, the whole thing. They put an ad in the paper and they got 450 guys who came in. They cut it down.

I was signed to Columbia Pictures at the time because I was in *Oliver!* on Broadway. They saw me, and they signed me up quick, and then kept me waiting for three years.

The Monkees came along, I auditioned like everybody else.

Now Bert Schneider, Bob Rafelson — the producers of *The Monkees* TV show — they thought, "Why should we go and find a group that has been playing in the Cavern, or wherever it is?" Most groups, they played for years, they toured with other people, they played with other people, and all the group waits for is somebody to come along and say, "You've got it! I'm going to put my money behind ya!" The green stuff, the money, that's all the group waits for. Well, Bert Schneider, Bob Rafelson *had* the money, they had a couple of thousand dollars or whatever it was hanging around, they went out and they got the cream of the crop, so they thought. They got the best four guys they could get out of 450. They looked at people in England, they looked at people all over the place, they wanted four entirely different personalities — not a rock and roll group — so that if my head was in the sand and my feet were sticking out they'd know it was me... because I'd be, like, eight inches shorter than the rest of them! But, you know, we're all different sizes, and we look different.[434]

*

The Monkees idea came out of me seeing the Byrds and Sonny and Cher at a place called Ciro's on Sunset Strip during 1965. I was in a penthouse across the street and I saw the Byrds and thought, I want that group to back me, I wanna be in a group. At the same time, Ward Sylvester, a friend of Bert Schneider and Bob Rafelson, took to them an idea for a show to be called The Monkees. Columbia Pictures was starting to falter a little because of union problems so they started merging and bringing independent companies in. Bert wanted to do his own thing so he brought Bob in and got Larry Tucker and Paul Mazursky to write a script. Then Ward, Bob, Bert and I went out and experienced the new groups — we really liked Arthur Lee and Love, and the Lovin' Spoonful. We needed three other guys for the show so we went to all the clubs in L.A. We found Micky playing with the Missing Links. Yes, there was a press ad, that's how we found Mike.[435]

*

To get things rolling, Ward [Sylvester] and I would go around to different clubs looking for prospective members for the TV show. We saw Sonny and Cher and The Byrds on one bill, and across the street was little Stevie Wonder. We went to see Arthur Lee and Love — this is all in one night. The guitar player from Love, a tall, good-looking blond guy, we thought would be good for the show. The Monkees vests and yellow shirts that we wore in our pilot came from what Sonny Bono was wearing. We saw the MFQ — the Modern Folk Quartet — with Chip Douglas; we looked at Jerry Yester as a potential candidate. Word was getting around, and people like Paul Peterson and Paul Williams, and actors from across the country were buzzing about this. They decided to have open auditions, so they put the Madness ad in Variety:

Madness!! Musicians, singers for acting roles in a new TV series — spirited Ben Frank's-types.

Ben Frank's was a restaurant on Sunset, a late night place to get your eggs and bacon after you've been out on the razzle. And so Ben Frank types were long-haired, sort of beatnik weirdos from the sixties. During the day it was a normal, eggs-over-easy place. But at night, it was a hangout, like Canters down on Fairfax Avenue. Bert wanted strange types; he wanted raw, new stuff that he alone could bring in. He's a strange old bird.[436]

*

Well, there was about four hundred and fifty people actually auditioned for this, and they sort of asked you weird questions and dug into your past and what your idea of the future for yourself was going to be. They were cruel.

Bert and Bob were very, very cruel. In fact, they were cruel to us, and we got the parts.

[The line in *Daydream Believers the Monkees Story*: *"Where did you get those stupid boots? Did you lose a bet?"]*

That kind of stuff. They were always like that though.

Once they got the show going, my reading on the whole thing was they *could* have used *any* one of those four people other than Micky, Mike, Peter, and myself. They narrowed it down to about twelve people and started sort of pairing us all up at the auditions, and I don't know whether it was a fluke that Micky, Mike, Peter, and I were the ones that ended up together in the end, but we did. It worked.

Bert Schneider actually was quite a passive kind of a guy. He was laid back, but I think that was the brand of coffee he was drinking. I'm not quite sure.

My reading anyway on Schneider and Rafelson was because I'd come into the flock with the pre-auditions, and they wanted fresh, new, they wanted it all to be *them*. They wanted to make the choices, and when I was there as a contract player from Columbia Pictures, and I had been for a number of years, they didn't really, fully, hundred percent go with the idea of *me* being in it. I felt that at the time, and I even said to my manager, "Let me reconsider this one. I don't think maybe this is the right thing for me."[437]

*

1962, I was on Broadview. I was playing the Artful Dodger in *Oliver!*. It was very difficult in those days to go from Broadway to television, and it wasn't something that people endorsed. I think the first person to really go from the Broadview stage, even into records, was Barbara Streisand, she made the transition. But I think *The Monkees* was more theatre, it was more

The Marx Brothers than it was The Beatles. The only thing we didn't do that The Three Stooges did, we didn't actually *hit* each other, so that's why I say Marx Brothers. But basically what we did, and this was true, before we started filming *The Monkees*, we actually sat and we watched *The Dead End Kids*, and *The Bowery Boys* and *The Marx Brothers*, and we did take improvisational classes. After seeing the TV show, obviously it didn't work, but you know, what can you do![438]

*

We would sit around for hours watching *The Marx Brothers*, *Three Stooges*, and *Laurel and Hardy*, learning comedy timing. We practised different accents and worked in different character roles so that when we were confronted by an unusual idea or situation in the show we had the reactions to it built in automatically. It was like putting a tape cassette into a machine. There were a lot of people depending on us, we had to know exactly what we were doing.[439]

*

I'd been working in New York in theatre. I was picked up by Columbia Pictures, and they were looking for something that I could be a part of. I did an audition for *Wackiest Ship In The Army*, and *Hogan's Heroes*, and I almost was Robin in *Batman*, but I didn't want to be wearing those tights. Then *The Monkees* idea came along, basically because of *A Hard Day's Night*, The Beatles, America's answer to the idea. So we filmed the show and it was quite an event because none of us had ever met before. You get put together and it works and you click and it's attractive to the viewer.[440]

*

As we started to film the TV show in the beginning, we obviously had to suss each other out, like normally you do within a relationship, and to me it was just another cast, another company, three other people that I was taking part in this production with. But as it went along obviously it became more than that, because this is despite being on Broadway and having experienced television in England and some other stuff, this was something *different* and you could *feel* it was. I was also 19 years old, 20 years old, so I was full of the fun at the fair, and so are the other guys.[441]

*

A one-word description of each of The Monkees.

Mike: big.

Micky: funny.

Peter: brainy.[442]

*

The friendships that Mickey, Peter, Mike and I had, they're all individual, different obviously, because we were all different characters. And that was the reason why we got our jobs as Monkees; they wanted four guys to be completely different. Mike was from Texas, Micky was from California, Peter was from Connecticut, and I was from England, and what they said was, if you put your head in the sand and your bums sticking up in the air then we'd know who it was. And that was basically it. We're all different looking, different characters.[443]

*

We were on our way down to shoot the pilot and get to know each other on the way, and I wanted to stop at a seafood restaurant, a place that was a little less greasy.

It was a learning process. It was like waking up every day and getting to know these guys, and that was all the way through the shooting. It was like two years of doing it.[444]

*

They sent us down to this town called Del Mar to film the pilot episode. We all travelled in the same car so that we could get to know each other, but there was no rapport at all, we just sat in the car looking out the window. It was Bert and Bob's idea and it made sense, all of us travelling like a theatre troupe. It was on the way down that I became aware of Micky's table manners, which were the worst in the world. He eats like it's his last meal and when he finishes with his plate it has to be thrown away because there are chips out of the bottom of it.

Now I couldn't believe this so I said to him, "I've never seen anybody eat like that in my life, man. You're a pig."

Suddenly a dead silence came over the table.

Mike looked at me, then Peter looked at me, and they were obviously thinking, "What's going on with this little Manchester jockey; where's he coming from?"

They all slowed right down because they were a little worried about their own table manners. What was I going to get upset about next?

So, I started cutting up the salad on my plate. Three minutes went by, it felt like ten. I put the dressing on, and they were all just staring at me. Then I put my knife and fork down, grabbed two handfuls of this chopped salad and rubbed it all over my face.

Well, that cracked them all up and it kind of broke the ice; we all felt a bit looser after that.[445]

*

It's like anything; like getting to know your wife. It's OK when you're engaged, looking like it's all gonna be roses. But then you realize she's untidy, or snores, or whatever. You don't determine any of that stuff.[446]

*

Micky and I had an apartment together in Benedict Canyon soon after that, so we were friends as much as you are at work, and then you go home. Sometimes you spend more time with them than you do even with your husband, your wife, or your kids, yet you don't hang out unless it's a special occasion, a birthday party, Christmas Eve, New Year party. So we weren't that close, but we were as professionals. We supported each other and helped each other, and so I guess it was a bit of each of those worlds.[447]

*

I don't know if [Peter and Mike] wanted to be the next Beatles, but they wanted to be taken seriously as musicians. Micky and I had [friends] that joined forces every weekend and went swimming in either their pool or my pool, and we played baseball with the Alice Cooper All-Stars every weekend.[448]

*

We all had our own private individual times with our friends. When we did get together it was on a Sunday afternoon, where Micky, me, Peter, and a bunch of other people, the stand-ins, and people we knew, we'd go out to the Valley in Los Angeles, play softball. And we'd then go to Micky's pool and swim, and then as the years went on — in '68, '69 — there was children involved and families and all this kind of stuff.

More the three of us, than Mike.[449]

*

As we got to know each other, we would get together on Sundays at Hazeltine Park in the Valley and have a baseball game. Peter would show up with his entourage and they all looked like flower power, it was like they were skipping around the maypole all the time. Then you've got Micky with his family, and then I'd be there with my girlfriend or, later, my wife. We'd have a great time, and then we'd all go back to Micky's or Peter's house and swim in the pool. Michael never joined us.[450]

*

I always wanted brothers. This is what I thought in the beginning. I thought it was gonna be like that. I thought: here we go now, this is gonna be all for one, and one for all. And it was until it got a little more successful.[451]

*

We used to fight like brothers. But all in all, I think I'd do anything for any one of them. I'd do anything I had to to help in any way I could, because once you've bonded and you've had this thing, such as The Monkees, to me, a friend is a friend for life. But this was *more*. This was finding three brothers I never had.[452]

*

To me, they were just other actors; other people that were in the same show. I never really got to know them, even to this day.[453]

*

Schneider and Rafelson — they kept us separate. Divide and conquer, that was their motto. That was their way of doing things.[454]

*

They really didn't get along, these three guys [Rafelson, Schneider and Kirshner], and Schneider having his father being the [studio] boss, I don't know what was going on internally. But he was always: my idea or nobody's. That was each one of those guys. They never compromised.[455]

*

Because we were fresh — we weren't friends before it started, we were just four guys put together, we had to find out about each other as well — so therefore, when we were discussing and talking, there was nothing set, there was no set return, it wasn't as if we rehearsed for six months and then we did a TV show, we just did a TV show; we'd only met *months* before. They put us all together and off we went. [It was fresh and spontaneous] and that's the way it was all the way through — it was for the first year.[456]

*

When we were working together, and we were doing stuff, it was great fun. It's the down times — and I think you'll find this with most entertainers — the down times are the hardest. And we just did a lot of pantomime, what we call English pantomime, which is like kids theatre, and that was basically what *The Monkees* was. I mean, *The Monkees*, to me, was just like a stage show. We could quite have easily taken it and put it live on a stage, and that's how improvised — the improvisation of the whole thing — a lot of this dialog was not written. A lot of the stuff we did was not written. It was just like *worked* around. We worked around it. They gave us like a premise, an idea of what to do.[457]

*

It was just a part that I was playing. I pretty much liked it, it was an easy role, I had thought that I was quite the lad when I was at school and in my teenage years I felt that I was just as much in the running as any other lad, after the girls, and then it went onto the screen. Living the fantasy. Sort of like the Artful Dodger, there was always a little bit of the Artful Dodger in me. When I was a kid, I was always captain of the cricket team and the football team and I could run faster than anybody else and throw a cricket ball farther than anybody else in my year. I always felt like that sort of cavalier type of chap. So *The Monkees* was an extension of that, I just got to play *myself* on screen, other than the fact that *that* was the place I got the girl![458]

*

To me, it was just another part. When I first started doing the show, I was very serious, and then I realised that these guys were getting all the laughs, you see! So I thought, I'd be a bit funny, too. And we had the people who were involved with the boom… we had the guy in the show that was holding the boom, and the makeup people were in the show, so it was great! We had everybody involved.[459]

*

It was too intense. The days were filled with being a Monkee. From 6:00 in the morning when my alarm went off, to the time I got in my car down Sunset Boulevard at 6:30, quarter to 7:00, get on the set 7:15, start to get made up and the show was being filmed at 8:00, if we weren't laughing.

We started laughing sometimes and we'd be laughing until 10:00 and they'd have to close the set down and we'd have to come back at 12:00. We had so much fun.

We had sound men helping with electrical cables. We had the prop man in the scenes doing a prop. It was a different Hollywood. There were certain union rules, and it's important to have rules and certain procedures, but it was the free form that spilled off the stage into the people surrounding us. We had a lovely family of people working with us. And that's why we kept the free form that we had for the first year.[460]

*

There were people pulling cables who weren't meant to be. There were ideas from the soundman, the boom man; we had the prop man playing a part, a real family situation.[461]

*

I remember the sound man moving electrician's cables and the electrician helping the prop man. And the prop man being in one of the scenes, and nobody from Actors Equity complaining. We all knew Micky Dolenz and myself being the actors, and Peter and Mike being the musicians. We did end up to be four musicians and four actors. We knew how to cover for each other. We saved time by being there, ready to film. The Monkees episodes went out for $75,000. I mean that's all they cost. That was unheard of. And that was because of the co-operation and the excitement and because of the originality and the enthusiasm from all these different areas.[462]

*

Kirshner, when he came in, he was really a very important man in the music business, and Micky did actually pour a glass of water over his head, not really knowing how important he was to everybody.

But he really was Mr. Music. He was the guy that everybody took their tunes to, because he had the access to a lot of artists that required tunes. The problem was, soon after The Monkees, most of the groups were doing their own songs and singing their own material, so you got Carole King and Neil Diamond, Harry Nilsson, Neil Sedaka, Carole Bayer-Sager, Leiber and Stoller, Barry Mann, Cynthia Weil, Tommy Boyce and Bobby Hart, all these guys came into their own at the time, because they had songs that they'd written that nobody was doing. When all the groups started to do their own material, then there was no place for them to place their tunes until The Monkees came along. Over the years, when I look back and read some of the comments from some of the songwriters, Neil Diamond, Carole King: "I wish I'd done it", "Anybody could have done it", or whatever they said. I mean, it's really backhanded, after the success we'd given them. One hand feeds the other.[463]

*

The pressure was definitely on Micky Dolenz, Mike Nesmith, Peter Tork and myself, because we were the guys that had to pull it off and take it to the public. The songs were written basically for the TV show, and then after the first album, they started bringing in other song writers, so people started to have an outlet for their songs. In the mid-sixties most bands were singing their own material, so all these song writers were sitting around twiddling their thumbs because all the bands were doing their *own* material. So all of a sudden there was a place for them to put their material and The Monkees was one of those avenues.[464]

*

Everybody thought we were an overnight success — Peter was in the Village for eight years plunking on his banjo; Mike was touring Texas, playing. They say we couldn't play, we can't play our own music, which was kind of funny. Micky had been in every group in town.[465]

*

Well [Last Train to Clarksville] was the first record The Monkees ever had on the radio. Micky Dolenz and I were driving along in Hollywood, and when that song was played on the radio we almost went through the roof! And there wasn't even a sunroof in the car! But we got so excited, it was on the radio six weeks before the show came on the air. So what came first, the chicken or the egg?[466]

*

Wh**W**hen I first heard "Last Train to Clarksville", I was with Micky Dolenz, driving down Benedict Canyon in Los Angeles in his Mustang. He had a green Mustang, a fastback, and we just stopped the car when we heard "Clarksville" on the radio for the first time. This was before it was a hit. We were together. It was unbelievable. I guess it was like being in a college dorm half the time, you know, just having to consider other people and… so many roommates.[467]

*

We lowered the age at which kids bought records. No kids ever bought Sinatra records but fourteen-year-olds bought The Beatles. We lowered the age to twelve.[468]

*

The producers wanted to see if we could perform music in front of an audience. They had Dick Clark book us in Hawaii, so that if we were lousy, no one would know — it's all those miles across the sea. Not only did we go to Hawaii for our first concert, but we played at the Miss Teenage American Beauty Pageant, which had an audience already built-in. We didn't have to sell tickets. I think we played half a dozen tunes, including "I'm A Believer," "Last Train to Clarksville," and "I Wanna Be Free." And they went crazy. The record that was number one in Hawaii was not "Last Train to Clarksville" but the B side, "Take A Giant Step." Because there were no trains in Hawaii, they turned the record over. We all hung out in a hotel and we met some interesting people, including Yevgeny

Yevtushenko, a Russian poet, who was there as the funny man in the entourage. I met my first wife there.[469]

*

One other thing I'm truly looking forward to — I can't wait to show people what we (The Monkees) can do in person. I guess it's an ego thing, but I'm really looking forward to going on tour.

To perform live is like nothing else. To have 3,000 girls screaming for you must be a good feeling — like riding a winner and listening to the crowd cheering![470]

*

We were rehearsing, rehearsing, rehearsing. We were a good band, and I'm not well impressed by many bands, but I was very impressed by the way we played together. And not just because I was in it. We *did* play good together.[471]

*

We did a lot of concerts. We weren't the greatest band in the world. In fact, when we played the national anthem, people from every country stood up, so, what can I say?[472]

*

I loved the concerts because that's where the live music for me was, and I was so proud of these guys, because they were so, so good! I'd never really been in a rock and roll band. I'd never really known how good a musician should be, but to me, they were great. They were top of the heap. But for those guys, it had to be all or nothing.

The concerts were absolutely wild. We couldn't hear a thing. There was never anything you could hear. You couldn't hear *nothing*. And that was always my fun time, when they said that I could get up and play the drums. I wasn't a drummer either, but I certainly could play "Stepping Stone".[473]

*

I couldn't play the drums because they couldn't see me behind them![474]

*

Our concerts were always just crazy. Didn't matter if you could play or not, because you couldn't hear a thing! We talked to each other on the stage, and it didn't really matter. The sound was coming out of amplifiers that were just regular amps on the stage. There were no speakers in the auditorium. If you ever heard The Beatles at Shea Stadium, you know what I'm talking about. The shirts are a direct steal from a John Wayne movie.[475]

*

This was the most exciting time, and always is, when we all hold hands and do our little bow together. We did it at the Greek Theater back in '87, '88 when we played there, all four of us on stage.[476]

*

Jimi [Hendrix]? He was a cool guy. Spent many an evening, just with him, went fishing with him in Miami, Florida, out on a boat for a day and a half. Just a regular guy, really. I had no idea what was going on in their personal lives, and I didn't really much care.

There was one occasion where Micky walked into a room where Stephen Stills and Hendrix was there, Joni Mitchell was there, Graham Nash was there, and they were playing and singing and strumming away, and Micky walked in and started banging sticks on the sideboard or on the table, and I remember quite distinctly Hendrix saying, "*That's* what we needed". So I mean, that was like a little smile on your face, you know? A *Monkee* playing with *Hendrix?* And he *liked* it?[477]

*

Some girl came up with an album and said, "Will you sign this?"

And we went, "What is *that?*"

She said, "It's your new album!"

It was *More Of The Monkees*; we were dressed in JC Penney clothes…[478]

*

When we talked about the war, we'd say, "Well, we're not soldiers, you know."

When we talked about drugs, we said, "Well, yeah, we drink Coca-Cola."

But *that* question kept coming up about, "You don't play. You can't do it."

Little did everybody know, neither did The Beach Boys. They didn't play in their studio sessions. The Association, The Turtles, The Byrds, believe it or not. Well, of course, all the other bands like Sonny and Cher, The Carpenters and all, they obviously used studio musicians. They had a group of musicians called The Wrecking Crew. The Wrecking Crew were five key musicians — Glen Campbell, Earl Palmer on drums, Larry Knechtel on bass, and just different great, great musicians. And if you look at albums from the sixties and seventies, you'll see these names all over the place. But this was a course that these guys held onto, and eventually, it destroyed our relationship with the studio, with each other. And Mike Nesmith was in the studio in '67, producing and doing his own stuff. Even then, he'd sorta started to separate himself.[479]

*

We were hired hands to start off with, and I had no idea that Mike Nesmith and Peter Tork would be so adamant about the music part.

I'd been signed to Columbia Pictures since 1963, and they had sent me to Hollywood. I auditioned for *Hogan's Heroes*, *The Wackiest Ship in the Army*, and *F-Troop*, and they wanted to put me in as Robin in *Batman* — all the stuff that was going on in the early '60s. So I never looked any farther than that. I thought *The Monkees* was a musical band, TV-show spin-off of *A Hard Day's Night*. It wasn't until I realized that Nesmith was driving a friggin' Eldorado and I had a Volkswagen that I realized he had all the B-sides with his material. He had quietly contributed more than we had in the studio, and was very adamant about not having to go in and be directed by [songwriters] Tommy [Boyce] and Bobby [Hart] or [producer] Donny Kirshner.[480]

*

Mike was a young adult, he was 22 years old at the time, and he had his own thing. It was very difficult, because I was a company man at the time. I'd already been part of the company for a number of years. I didn't really understand it, but being soldiers in arms… it was the first time I'd had brothers around me, and sort of school chums. I never really had to make decisions like that. My background was Broadway, and the theater had a discipline I was used to — being directed, produced and wardrobed and everything else. I'm a working actor, a theatrical performer, and that's all I cared about. I made $450 a week, then the second year we made $750, and we had songwriters, and people that did things that I didn't do. I've learned to do those things, so now I can do it, but I wasn't going to hold up operations because of that.[481]

*

There was a guy called Herb Moelis, who was the lawyer, and he got very aggressive in that meeting [with Kirshner]. He really upset Michael, and that's why he punched the wall. [Mike punched the wall and said to Moelis, "That could have been your face, Motherfucker!"]

It could have been a beam too, Michael! That would've hurt!

He was telling me, "I can sue you. Your name's on a piece of paper!" And, you know, we weren't used to being talked to this way, and Bert and Bob were not with us. They just sent us to the wolves at this point. I had no idea why.

And I left with Lester Sill, the second in command (who became the first in command because Donny Kirshner was fired), and as we walked out of there, we looked at each other and I said, "This is it. This is the end, isn't it?"

He said, "I think it is".[482]

*

Chip Douglas was very instrumental in grounding all of us. He was very instrumental in grounding us all. He took us in and produced us when we did the *Headquarters* album. He brought good songs to us like, "Steam Engine", "Toys", and especially "Daydream Believer". This kicked us off again in '68. This was our really last major, major, major, major hit, and I think one of the more remembered songs. What you do *last* is usually the way people think about you.[483]

*

We had a lot of good people around us. It wasn't just the four of us. Although, we were pretty much overlooked as far as being responsible (other than surface) for the success. We *did* work together. We *did* help each other. We *did* try to improve on everything we did, and when we got involved with Chip on this particular album [*Headquarters*], we started making these songs, it was a lot more earthy than a lot of the stuff we'd done. We actually *felt* like a band during the recording of this particular album. We went in a few times later, but basically, what would happen was they'd get a song, and they'd say, "Oh, there's a song, 'I'm a Believer' or 'Daydream Believer' or 'Valleri' or 'Pleasant Valley'", and they'd pretty much either give it to me, or give it to Peter… Mike really turned down singing tunes. He didn't want to sing other people's tunes even. So it was very difficult trying to satisfy everybody. When you've got four celebrities, four personalities — all for one, one for all was great when we were all together — but then everybody went over to their little worlds and we somewhat forgot about each other.[484]

*

We actually played our own instruments. In a sense, we became our own cover band. None of the bands of the 60's were playing on their own records. The Beach Boys never played on "Good Vibrations", McCartney didn't play the French horn on "Penny Lane". Even though *The Monkees* was a TV show about a band, we actually turned into a full-out band.[485]

*

Favourite album was *Pisces, Aquarius, Capricorn and Jones, Ltd*, and it wasn't just because I had a song on it — it was "Hard to Believe", a song I wrote with a couple other guys that walked in the room at the time.[486]

*

It was interesting that we all jelled and blended right away, knew what was right, knew what was wrong, got on with the job, fooled around all the time. The guest artists were going, "Who *are* these guys?"

The first time we got together as The Monkees, we all sat down around the table, like normally you do when you're starting a show in the morning, you know: Monday morning you will read through the scripts, and then you make notes and you take stuff out and you do this, that and the other. Well that happened for about two Monday mornings. And after that there was none of that. It was just: get in there, do the dialogue, change certain words around — from *groovy* to *cool*.

In fact in "Daydream Believer", John [Stewart] had, "Now you know how *funky* I can be."

And I went, "*Funky*? I don't think this is going to hold up."

So we actually changed it. "Now you know how *happy* I can be."[487]

*

I didn't know what I was singing. When we did "Daydream Believer", Chip Douglas, who produced it, came to me, and he said, "Well, what do you think about that one?" because we had 12 songs, and this was the 13th song.

I said, "Yeah. Dump that."

He said, "No. This is a single."

I said, "I don't know…"[488]

*

We'd done twelve songs, and the thirteenth was "Daydream Believer".

I said, "That's terrible."

I was a baritone and it was in the wrong key for my voice. I'd been in the studio all day, I was tired, and I'm singing these words about twelve times, "Cheer up, sleepy Jean. Oh, what can it mean to a daydream believer and a homecoming queen."

I kept asking Chip what the words meant, and he said, "Don't worry, just sing them."

I said, "Okay… I'll sing it until I get it right."

So Chip says, "All right, one more time, 'Daydream Believer.'"

And I started it, and I failed, and I failed, and I failed.

Hank Cicalo, the engineer, had his own way of numbering takes so he could find them; he'd call them 1A or 2A, like that. Anyway, all of a sudden, he says "7A" over the talkback, and I wasn't listening so I said, "What number is this?"

And they said, "7A!" in unison.

That kicked me on a bit, and I got it down, but you can tell from the vocal that I was pissed off.[489]

*

We very often did have a say [in the songs The Monkees would record], and we very often did *not* have a say. For example, we turned down Neil Sedaka's "Love Will Keep Us Together", and the song "Knock Three Times On The Ceiling If You Want Me".

I said, "I'm not singing *that*. You must be joking."[490]

*

And the thing about The Monkees' songs, if you really care to take time to listen down to some of the albums that we did, it's all so different. It wasn't just any one particular style. You could definitely know and understand that it was The Monkees that was doing it. But with all these different songwriters you'd think that there'd be some kind of separation in style. But I think as soon as The Monkees did it, then it became, you know, a Monkees *sound*, even though it was Neil Diamond and Carole King and all the other great songwriters. And this was a fun time.[491]

*

W e only want what is due to us. Our last tour grossed two million, but we only made a tiny percentage of that. Something has to change. We are a film-making group that has got into a music groove. What I'd really like to do with the boys is a Broadway musical. With the acting and musical experience between us we could have a smash and be the first group to do it. Or we could do a whole show at the London Palladium.[492]

*

I f people here on the British pop scene really knew how hard we work on the set for those Monkee programs, they'd never put us down. Half the time we're so tired that we're on doctor's shots to keep us going. All this didn't come about overnight — there's been a lot of hard work involved for us all. I've never claimed to be a pop star. I'm an actor, and the public has made me a rock and roll singer. Now I'm pleased about that. It's brought me a lot of good things and I'm still new enough to all this success to enjoy the crowds, the autograph hunters and the adulation. Maybe when I've had it for as long as The Beatles — if I'm that lucky — then I'll be tired too.[493]

*

O ur wardrobe man was a guy called Gene Ashman. We had this one guy who designed most of our clothes, and pulled a bit from here and there. This outfit — the corduroy pants, the yellow shirt, and the little Monkee waistcoat — the outfit itself was a direct steal from Sonny Bono. He was wearing that when he was with Cher in the beginning when they were playing together.[494]

*

We didn't date ourselves with any particular styles. Obviously, you see bell-bottom pants coming out, and certain trends of the Nehru collars and all this kind of stuff. We never had an authority in our TV show where we had a manager or a parent or somebody telling us what to do, so that was attractive. We were on the beach in an old house, and so it still had the same look and people are still decorating their houses that way — throw together bits and pieces or anything you can find — not conventional, just make it all mix and match.[495]

*

We all dressed as girls eventually. We all put the dress on, and the wig, and the whole thing. I thought Nesmith was so funny in ["The Fairy Tale Episode"]. He *was* funny, you know. He just didn't allow himself to enjoy it. That was the problem. Many a time they'd close the set down, because we just kept laughing, and laughing, and we couldn't do it. So we laughed so much, they said if, "Okay, if you don't do it this time, we're closing down until after lunch, and this was at nine-thirty in the morning. I swear. It's the truth.[496]

*

You've seen these clips they show on television shows where the people start laughing and they're kibitzing and they can't do their lines? Well, that's what it was like on our show all the time. In fact, one day, you will not believe it. We came in — we used to start filming about 7:30, 8 o'clock. Well, at 9 o'clock the stage floor man said, "Okay, that's it! Come back after lunch; you're finished!" We were laughing so much, we couldn't do it![497]

*

When I was late for filming one morning, and a guy wanted my ID. I didn't have it, and he wouldn't let me in the gate.

I told him, "You better let me in, otherwise I'm gonna blow through here!"

And I did. And about a foot of it went up and down all day long after that, until they fixed it the next day.[498]

*

When we got that incredible raise, it was obvious that more was expected of us, we had to become more professional.[499]

*

After about the first season, there was this noise that they had to get rid of on the set — and it was the four of us in our little dressing rooms! So they took the dressing rooms off the set, which were like these little cabins, and they put us in a box at the back of the set. They knocked a hole in the wall, and we had a meat freezer cooler door on it. It was thick, about a foot thick, and you couldn't hear a thing. It had a light in each corner of the room; when they wanted me, they flashed this one, that one, the other one: me, and Micky, Peter. And we were out there playing, that's where our guests used to go: around the back door, and in the back of the studio. And it was quite amazing that we ever got anything done the second season. Scripts kinda, in my opinion, just dropped off a little bit, but maybe that was to do with the guys. Maybe it was to do with us. We weren't so animated and we had, now with the success, *more* responsibilities, personally and otherwise, to be able to cope with, as well as doing these shows. We were at the studio by six-thirty in the morning, and we'd leave the studio at five-thirty at night, and then Micky and I'd go into the studio and record, and that was what our life was for a good part of the time we were in The Monkees.[500]

*

We played all the time on the set. When we weren't filming, we were in a little room. A little black box, we called it. It was a soundproof room. We played *all* the time, you know. We just practiced and rehearsed, and although it was taped music when we were filming, it was not something we weren't working on, and we were working slowly towards all of us doing our own music. In a sense, *playing* our own music.[501]

*

They used the box, which was actually a room about 12'×16', to keep us out of the way, which was fine by us.

I'd be kissing one girl, going to another, saying, "Wait a minute, I'll be with you in a second."

Mike was on the phone making business calls and yelling at everyone.

Peter was saying, "More brown rice please, all over my nose so I can't breathe but can still read the Maharishi."

Micky was doing his: "aarghbrr-yes-no-why-how-come-go-zap-wow-up-down-more-less-aaargh" thing, burning off energy.[502]

*

I was in the Monkee mobile a number of times. Once I do remember going around Riverside Raceway, racing it — it only went to maybe 90 miles an hour and I had every one of those amps going and I think it was the last bend before the straight that I completely spun out onto the sand, and went round about four times, that thing jiggled, and I never drove it again![503]

*

We're on tour, in our hotel room, and there's a knock on our door. "Pizza's arrived."

We said, "We didn't order pizza, but we'll have it, please come in."

So they came in and they gave us the pizza. It's these two seventeen-year-old girls in pizza outfits with little hats, the whole thing. Then they finally told us: they'd actually ordered the pizza to their room, bribed the delivery guys for their outfits and that's how they got in. And we thought that was a very original idea.

When we toured, we used to take whole floors. We used to wall creep, used to creep along the walls and get into gaps in the doors, pretending we were shooting each other and doing all kinds of things you only do when you're on the road. Our fans were so young, there weren't mass orgies going on or anything. It was kind of weird; my love life was like the Petrified Forest.[504]

*

We had all these little games that we used to play, and one of them was called *Killer*. You had three lives. You'd call, "Hey, Micky!" and Micky would look and you'd go, "Bang!" Then he would have to fall and do a spectacular death, over chairs, whatever it might be.

We'd just arrived in Australia and we were walking down the steps of the plane. I made sure I got down to the bottom real quick, first. Micky's at the top and I said, "Micky!"

And he went, "Oh, no…"

I said, "Bang!"

He does this spectacular fall all the way down the steps and the fans are going, "Oh, poor Micky!"

You had three lives and that's all you had for the whole game, and once you lost your three lives, you were out of the game, forever. To get in the game was tough enough, so nobody wanted to be out. It was the four of us, Bert, Bob, Ward, Jack Nicholson, and James Frawley. I remember when the game was over and it was because of Frawley. The second season was coming to an end. We were fooling around on the set, and Frawley shot himself three times and that was the end of his game. The Killer game ended, like everything else ended.

We could feel it. "Hey, hey, we *were* The Monkees." It was coming to an end.[505]

*

There was an occasion in Memphis that was the most frightening of all. We were on our way out the rear of a hotel and we turned a corner to find ourselves confronted by about one hundred and fifty fans. We had three big strong bodyguards with us and the girls just trampled all over them.

We dived out a back exit and into a subway, which proved to be the year's biggest mistake because we rounded a corner there to find hundreds of fans on the way to our concert.

There we are running down the main street pursued by several hundred fans who are driving us toward the stadium, where there are approximately ten thousand more fans milling about outside who can't get seats.

Just as we were giving up hope, two police cars drew up alongside and we found ourselves running between them. Then they opened the doors and let us jump in — that's about the only time I've been really glad to see them.[506]

*

I would think [the show] broke ground; four long-hairs were on the television for a start. Once in a while you'd see a long-hair come through a movie, or a play of the week, or whatever it is, and he was either a beatnik, or a musician, or something.

I think that we did break ground with introducing old techniques that have been used before, we were likened to The Beatles' *A Hard Day's Night*. They said they took *A Hard Day's Night* and put it on television, but The Beatles weren't actors, they're not actors, they were just guys, musicians, romping around. They were doing romps, like *The Monkees* did Monkee romps, I think we did more innovative film techniques in our movie, *Head*.[507]

*

We did a movie called *Head*. Bob Rafelson, Bert Schneider, Jack Nicholson, Peter, Micky, Davy and Mike. We all wrote that. We didn't get credit for it, but we did write it. (Naughty men!) But that was their doing, you know. There's nothing we could do about it.[508]

*

But this was cool with Nicholson. [Jack] Nicholson came into the scene as a friend of Rafelson and Schneider. They'd worked together on projects pre-Monkees and probably didn't get them off the ground, and all of a sudden, they pulled him in, and Jack was much the same as Clint Eastwood. He'd been making spaghetti westerns and doing small parts here and there. If you looked through his roster of things he did way before he was "Jack Nicholson" to the world, you'll see some really funky stuff. At the time, they'd just finished making *Easy Rider*, and Schneider and Rafelson contributed $75,000 to finish the movie with Peter Fonda, and Jack was in it, and Dennis Hopper, and a number of other people, and they gave them $75,000 for, I think, two percent, three percent of the movie when it came out. Maybe it was more. And obviously, it made millions at the time, which was high grossing for an independent film. Especially with the content and the kind of storyline that it had.

Nicholson came into the scene. We all went off to Del Mar and we spent a weekend, three days, with a tape recorder, and we all threw our ideas out and decided where we wanted to go with it, what should we do with this. Everyone had different ideas. So we took the four personalities: Micky was funny man, he just like joked the whole thing; Peter was Hare Krishna, waterbeds, brown rice; Mike Nesmith was the businessman; and I was the guy, "Who said that? I'll punch him!" Being a little guy, I was a little feisty and sort of always in the mix.

But we all got together for a weekend — Schneider, Rafelson Nicholson, Nesmith, Tork, Jones, and Dolenz — and we all sat and talked, wrote our ideas, taped them. I would love to have that tape right now. I'd love to listen to that tape, because there was a lot of stuff obviously that we didn't do. We all had ten ideas and only one of them was good. These guys really, you know, it was a bit of a joke. I mean, we were using people's money to make a movie, not a lot, I think they spent about a couple hundred thousand dollars. Each episode of *The Monkees*, if you can believe it, cost thirty-five thousand dollars, which was ridiculous.[509]

*

The idea of the *Head* movie was that we had to break out of the black box, which represented *life*. We all had different ways of getting out. Mike's way was to talk his way out, because he's the business man. Peter, Hare Krishna, water beds, brown rice, was to sort of levitate yourself out of the box. Micky was a jokester, and I had to fight my way out because I was always feisty. Being shorter than most, I always had to push my way forward. I had to let people know I was there.[510]

*

We didn't show up for the first day's filming. Micky, Mike, and myself. Peter showed up. And if you look at the movie now, you'll see that Peter has a swollen face. He has a nose on him. He'd got bitten by a bee over the weekend or something. He was the only one that showed up, because by this time, Mike Nesmith had gotten Jerry Perenchio to be Micky, mine, *and* his agent, you see. The manipulation was beginning, and the separation had already begun. Peter was Bert Schneider and Bob Rafelson's friend more than he was ours. It's quite interesting how the events came about. Lot of music, lot of traveling, a lot of work. Very little time to really spend on your personal life, and I think that was the hardest thing about being in The Monkees that I wasn't able to really have any long-term relationships during that period. That would last anyway. It's all happened since. And obviously my school friends before and at home.[511]

*

One of the most challenging things to happen to me lately is the opportunity to do a big production number in the forthcoming Monkee movie. My number is called "Daddy's Song" and it's going to be a real big Broadway-type song and dance number. I have been rehearsing so hard that I lost five pounds! I hope you see the movie and think it was worth it![512]

*

There was an unusual amount of tension in the air as I went onto Stage 7 at Screen Gems today. A great array of music play-back equipment had been wheeled onto the stage and the entire Monkee production staff — minus all The Monkees but me — had gathered on the set to watch today's shooting.

As I strode across the large set towards my dressing room, everyone said, "Hi!" and I waved back — but things weren't as they usually were. I was trying to figure out who was more nervous — me or the crew? Today was probably the most important day in my entire show-business career: today was the day we began to film the big musical production number I perform in The Monkees' new movie. I had chosen the song called "Daddy's Song", not because it's sentimental (in fact, it's quite the contrary, so don't misinterpret it when you hear the lyrics), but because it's such a good tune that I feel it will be an instant hit.

All last week, The Monkees costumer Gene Ashman and I had worked together designing two groovy outfits for me to wear in this sequence. One is a black tuxedo with a long, flared jacket, and the other is a white tuxedo styled exactly the same way. With the black tuxedo, I wear a white shirt — and with the white tuxedo, I wear a black shirt. The two shirts are exactly the same design, ruffled at the neck, cuff and down the front. They're almost a line-for-line copy of the beautiful yellow batiste shirt Gloria Stavers had made for me and gave to me a little over a year ago. That shirt, by the way, is still one of my favorites. I only wear it on special occasions.

While I was in the dressing room getting ready, choreographer Toni Basil came in to greet me. We had been rehearsing together for two weeks and now she explained to me that she thought it would take us (Toni appears in the movie in my big song-and-dance number with me) about two and a half days to shoot the "Daddy's Song" sequence. Those two weeks with Toni were real educational, let me tell you! I found out that it requires more effort to get into perfect physical shape to do a dance routine than it does for a jockey to get into shape to ride in races! Mr. Fred Astaire has my profound respect.

Our sets were designed in a very stark and unusual manner. During the first half of the song, I'm in black — so we dance on white tiles with totally white backdrops. During the second half, I switch to my white tuxedo — and then the tiles and backdrops turn black. The scene starts with me singing (the tune was written by Harry Nilsson) —

Years ago I knew a man,
He was my mother's biggest fan.
We used to walk beside the sea
And he told me how life would be
When I grew up to be a man.

Later on, the lyrics tell how this little boy's father left him (see, I told you it wasn't like my real life at all!), and the little boy gets bitter and decides that when he grows up his son will never know that sadness. I sing this song slow at first, and the only prop that enters is an umbrella which flashes on when I have one line, "*It was such a rainy day...*"

After I have sung the song slowly, Toni dances onto the set and we do our big duet together. I hope you like it, my little sunshines, cos your boy Davy lost ten pounds learning to get it all down just right for you! After the dance sequence, I suddenly appear in the white outfit and do the tune up-beat — and do a fast dance with it for the grand finale.

I think I got one of the finest compliments I have ever had in my relatively long show-business career when I was leaving the set. When everyone was finished, I went to my dressing room, changed to my own clothes and started to leave. As I walked out, one of the hairdressers — a lady who has been watching stars come and go at Columbia for the last 20 years — walked over to me. She placed her hands on my shoulders and said, "Davy, I have seen a lot of things in all the years I've been here, but the performance you just gave was one of the greatest things I've ever seen."

Then I saw that there were tears in her eyes. I really was speechless. So I leaned over and kissed her on both cheeks. We smiled at each other and I left.

It's a moment I'll never forget.[513]

*

The Monkee movie *Head* was a good movie. The only problem with it was that our fans couldn't get in to see it because it was rated for adults. So it was a movie that really should have been made at the time not with The Monkees. I was thinking more of like *Road to Hong Kong* [Bing Crosby, Bob Hope and Joan Collins, 1962] or sort of like *The Marx Brothers go to Beijing*. Instead of that, we made this controversial movie about the Vietnam War, and about philosophy, and as I say, we had four different ways of getting out of the black box. We used the black box. We used Victor Mature. We had Annette Funicello, Sonny Liston, Ray Nitschke from the Green Bay Packers. I mean, this was all conversations that we had during the course of this meeting, and that's how that movie came about.

They paid us a thousand dollars for doing the movie, and that was it.

And I guess that was it.[514]

*

That particular picture [The Ditty Diego sequence ending with real life footage of Nguyễn Ngọc Loan executing Nguyễn Văn Lém during the Vietnam War], that was what stopped the movie from being shown to a general audience, because they wouldn't take it out. That one little thing at the end, you know?

I'd always thought The Monkees were gonna make a movie similar to our show: a lot of fun, sort of like, you know, Chevy Chase on a summer holiday or... *Beach Blanket Bingo*, or whatever they called it with Sandra Dee and Bobby Rydell and all that. But no, we took the events of the time, which we'd been asked *not* to talk about. Drugs, we *never* talked about. Political opinions, we *never* talked about. And here, all of a sudden, it's like the top gets off the bottle, and all this comes out.[515]

*

I think there was some techniques in that movie that had never been used before; we used all kinds of stuff, and it's still used in theatre classes, and it's shown in art houses and at colleges and places. It is a cult film. It wouldn't have been my choice, The Monkees had a certain following, they were under fifteen, fourteen year olds, there were *some* older people that watched it also, but most of our fans were younger — that movie was *not* geared at those people, so I feel that we lost a lot of ground there by allowing that sort of movie to be made. But The Monkees were starting to fold up, as a unit.[516]

*

This would explain my feelings about Schneider and Rafelson.

We were playing dandruff in Victor Mature's hair, okay, in the Monkee movie *Head*. Dandruff. *Dandruff*! I think that's the value they put on us, to tell you the truth, and that would hold true with some of the things I've said so far about these guys.

They were never very helpful to us, other than they gave us the opportunity to do what we did. I guess *that* was everything.[517]

*

I saw it all change as the show went into the second season. People were late, and people weren't cooperating as much as they did, and we got different directors coming in. Instead of keeping the fun of the fair, we all let it overcome us, the success that was happening, and I think maybe we changed each other. And maybe changed the feeling that we had, the first season, of excitement: "Wow, this is great! Wow, look at that!"[518]

*

The second year everybody got just a bit too big for their britches: Micky wanted to direct; Mike wanted to produce; Peter wanted to write; I wanted to do all of those things. And so it got a bit sloppy. The second year of *The Monkees* series was not as strong as I believe the first year was, and this was the end coming faster than it should have had. Because if you're working for a company, they don't want to have the employees all of a sudden considering themselves for the production staff, or as director, producer, writer. You're hired to do a job. But it gets blown out of proportion because, when you sell 100 million records, and fans are screaming all over the place, at the gates and everywhere you go, you tend to lose a little bit of reality. And we were twenty, twenty-one, twenty-two, twenty-three years old, we were very, very young, and very unknowing of what was going on in the show business world.[519]

*

I was used to being with professional actors, so there's a way of conducting yourself. I used to hang out with Judy Garland, Elizabeth Taylor, Dudley Moore and Georgia Brown and all these people on Broadway. We used to go straight off to Jim Downeys or Sardi's Steakhouse. I was used to being around adults. And all of a sudden I was put with these three other boys. To me, it was always a job. I was playing the part of a rock and roll singer in a TV series. It gelled, and it worked for a long time, until Micky wanted to direct, and Mike wanted to write all the music, and Peter wanted to play on all the records. I probably was a pain in the ass, too. When everybody started to want to do everybody else's job, that's when it became the deck hands taking over the ship. Our immaturity flared. We didn't behave like big shots; we never went around saying, "Do you know who I am?" and driving Rolls Royces.[520]

*

I just didn't *get* any of this towards the end, and I was just a bit sort of confused as to why the pirates were taking over the ship, or not co-operating with what was obviously a successful thing for us, and so it was kind of sad.[521]

*

When you start getting Monkee pens and Monkee bubblegum, that's when the fun stops. Micky was still doing his. "You dirty rats," thing; I was still falling in love with the same girl. We decided to forget it, man.[522]

*

We were burned out with each other. *The Monkees* was never cancelled for a start. NBC wanted to do a third year. We said what we wanted to do is a sort of "Laugh In" thing, and this is before "Laugh In" came on.

We wanted to interview people on the show, do variety, get the artists, the guests, involved with us in our group. They wanted to keep the four guys together. We wanted to change the format. We wanted to present ourselves as individuals, and as a group, and as an improvisational group working with other people.[523]

*

We talked about doing a different format. Really, basically, what *Laugh-In* turned out to be. Like a variety show. We were getting guest artists on there, but in the second season Tim Buckley was on, and I had a guy called Charlie Smalls.

Charlie Smalls was the guy that wrote *The Wiz*, and I've got a tape of him in my living room in Hollywood, playing, "You can't win, you can't break even, can't get out of the game," and all the other songs from The Wiz. It's priceless. One day, I'm gonna hook up with his son. I haven't seen him in thirty-five years. Michael, his name was — and I've got videos of him as a little kid and everything. I understand he's a director in New York or producer or choreographer. I'll have to look him up and give him the tapes that I've got of his dad.[524]

*

Nothing has been laid out for us. We have no plans really. The only plans we have for this next year is that the TV show has been dropped; we could have gone another year, NBC said, "We'll pick you up and you can go another year," but the guys were fed up with doing the whole Beatle thing, and Dick Lester, and running around, and being funny. We want to do three specials to show that we're not just a rock and roll group that stands up and plays; we're an *act*. We can't *only* do little skits on the TV. The Marx Brothers were doing it ten years ago, so The Beatles and Dick Lester weren't the first, there was somebody before The Marx Brothers I should think, Three Stooges or whatever.

We can only go as far as the public will take us — the people that are paying the money to see us all, the people that want to look at us on the TV — we can only go as far as they want us to go. What I'd *like* to do, I'd like to stick with the guys as long as I can, but no matter what I do, I'm sure that they're always going to say (*if* they say, "That's David Jones!") they're going to say, "That's David Jones, you remember that David Jones from The Monkees?" Whether I'm sitting in a cafe drinking a cup of coffee with a heavy beard on my face, out of work, they're still going to say that.

I'd like us to get into Broadway shows and things like that, the four of us, and come on [stage], maybe play rock and roll for five or six songs, do twenty minutes of skits. We'll take a theatre for six weeks and instead of doing a monstrous concert and having ten thousand kids there screaming, we'll have four thousand adults in the audience because they want to see some of The Marx Brothers, or they want to see some of the Dick Lester, Beatle things. And we'll have a variety show, we've got to bring variety back because it's slowly dying out, and I think that's where everybody's got to go; you've got to go to the more personal feeling in show business because that's what works.

People want something new and fresh and different, they don't want the same boloney they've heard. So an actor or a performer has to *change,* he has to change with the people. That was the reason we made it in the beginning, because the kids that were supporting The Beatles, eight-year-olds, they started between eight and eighteen — big age group they got — now the kids that were five at the time couldn't go for The Beatles because they were too old. Three years later when we came out they were eight years old and they've got something.[525]

*

I don't really know if I hope one day I'll be on my own, because I tried for six years on my own. I really don't [want to] split from the guys; if it happens, it happens, that's the way it's going to be, but I don't really foresee anything on my own yet. Not within the next three years.

I hope that in three years from now that I'll still be with the guys, because we've had a good time together, and if we didn't enjoy one another we wouldn't be here now.[526]

*

My only regret about *The Monkees* is that I wish we'd gone on for another year. I don't think the quality was dropping. It could have gone on because we had the potential. We could have hosted TV shows, the four of us with guests.[527]

*

We all had these suits, you know. I guess that's a spin-off once again of The Beatles, the suits and ties and stuff. We got them from around the corner of the studio. There was this shop. We used to go in there and order a four hundred dollar pair of boots. I'll put it on the bill, you know, thinking that that was that. But wow, it all came out in the end! They took the cars back, the bikes, the clothes, everything.[528]

*

After the show went off the air nobody wanted anything to do with us.

One day we were so hot and the next day all the doors were shut and we were standing in the cold all alone.[529]

*

I stayed last night at the Del Coronado, which is where we shot *The Monkees* pilot, and that running up and down on the beach (like the little birds do) was all at the Del, and when I went there yesterday, I got goosebumps because it had been many years since I'd been there (about 45 actually), and I saw that metal elevator and the little man standing there — I think it was the same guy — and I thought, "Well, we're both looking pretty good!" No, it was quite a happy memory because it was all part of that connection — during those days it was Peter Fonda and Jack Nicholson and many other people that were involved around our little project and so we got a lot of input from a lot of people, it wasn't just the studio or Micky, Mike, Peter, and myself, it was a collaboration of many, many, many that were stolen or plagiarised from The Beatles or *A Hard Day's Night*.[530]

*

Well, we broke up as a unit, but as a show it's just gone on and on and on.[531]

*

Everything since [The Monkees] I've done myself. My life has basically been a springboard from The Monkees.[532]

*

When we get together a magical thing happens — for all of us. Call it whatever you want — crap, manufactured, whatever.

What we call it is: great fun.[533]

*

Even now, with The Monkees, I'm not looking for stardom. I've bought my father a house and I'd like to make some more money to set up a business in England. In about ten years I'd like to be directing, working here six months of the year and six months in England. I'd also like to go round the world someday.[534]

*

Micky, Peter and I are going to do a TV special; we're also writing a movie over the next couple of months, and recording, so it's a very active life for a guy in mid-life. We're all having a great time, enjoying each other's company [2001].[535]

*

I would like to see *The Monkees Save the World*. I'd like to see a *Monkees Ghostbuster*. I would like to see *The Monkees in Lost Paradise* or *The Three Musketeers* or whatever. The Monkees shouldn't have to be explained at this point. They should be entertaining, just four guys running around. We need to get involved in some fun fantasy and drama. We know they live in a Malibu Beachhouse and do gigs. I've written a script too, which is a play on the TV show. We go to the jungle and go through all kinds of adventures. Otherwise we'll look like four grumpy old men going on about what might have been. But the fans don't feel that way.[536]

*

I've always had people listen to me or look at me.

When I was a kid, they'd tap me on the head and say, "What a handsome boy."

So I always felt pretty special. People have treated me that way all my life. I'm very blessed. So I never had any thoughts of, "It's gonna get bigger, it's gonna get better." It's as big as it ever was.

I go through airports and there's always someone who shouts, "Hey, hey, we're The Monkees!" And that was 40 years ago. It's like being in the Mafia. Once you're in, you're in.[537]

*

Little story about this is that during this period of time, when we shot this movie [*Head*], at the airport, I hooked up with four soldiers that were going off to Vietnam, and just recently, I met one of them. Gave me a t-shirt with a picture of the four of them and me on it. I'd given them records before they left. They played them through their term over there, and even kept the picture all those years, forty years later.[538]

*

The Monkees went to about 36 countries; the show was dubbed in Japanese; we had a hit with "I'm a Believer" in Italian, we had a hit in Mexico with Micky singing Spanish, there was a lot more going on than ever was seen generally in one dimension. We had a heck of a career.[539]

*

We touched a lot of musicians. I can't tell you the amount of people that have come up and said, "I wouldn't have been a musician if it hadn't been for The Monkees." It baffles me even now. I met a guy from Guns N' Roses, and he was overwhelmed by the meeting and was just so complimentary.[540]

*

We have a big tour bus. We've all the videos and the movies — 300 satellite channel on there — a place to hang our clothes, and we all sit around at night, play some rummy and have a little chat, work on songs and stuff, so it's pretty cool.

Micky, Peter and I, we've been buddies for years, and every five or six years we get together, our schedules correspond, and we're able to work out some road sense. We don't actually get paid for doing what we do, we get paid to *travel*. That's the hardest part of the gig. For anyone who's on the road most of the time who's listening, it's very weary. You get very weary. It's very fatiguing, but our bonus is that we get thrown a "birthday party" every night.

The whole show lasts about three hours, with a small intermission in between so everybody can powder their noses and refresh themselves. It changes every night, those guys are so unpredictable, that's why I like to work with them, you know what I mean?

It's not as tense as I make it sound. It's a great fun idea. Micky and Peter and I, we're just laughing, all the time. We're still playing silly boy tricks on each other. None of us really grew up with our families, we were on the road and out doing stuff — my Broadway experience; Micky's directorial [career], he directed stage productions and TV; Peter's got his own band, Shoe Suede Blues — and so we are pretty active out of The Monkee's circle, but being in The Monkees is like the mafia, once you're in, you're in.

It's safe ground for us, we know each other so well, we've been out there doing our own thing for a couple of years, and now we're back together bringing to the table what we've learnt, and things we've experienced, and songs we feel worked, and ideas we want to present, and so everybody's open all the time — we all teach, and school each other continually, and that's why the success has happened for the last 35 years plus. This is no joke. The Monkees are, in some people's eyes, legendary figures. As far as we're concerned, we're just fellas who are still doing the same things they did all those years ago, and enjoying it, and fortunately we have more than one or two hits to be able to present to the audience, and that's a wonderful thing for us. Most acts go out there with one or two hits and the rest is filler, but we've got songs that people can sing along to.[541]

*

You've got to sing along. Because we're old; we forget the words.[542]

*

Now, I've said I'd never work with The Monkees again [2010], but I talked to Micky and Peter the other day quite sensibly, as adults, and there was an offer from some people: "We would like to take you to England, perform here, perform there…"[543]

*

But that's all water under the bridge. What happened in 2002 was that we were all tired, and when we're tired, we start arguing. As for Mike, I don't blame him for not touring.

When I started out in The Monkees, I was like: "Let's have fun and then I can go home, smoke a joint, and drink a beer."[544]

*

The fun of the fair is not over – The Monkees can still entertain and be the way they were. The skipping's not happening too much anymore, obviously![545]

*

We have a great time, it's like having a birthday party thrown for you every night. Mind you, we don't want those birthdays to come too soon anymore. Keep them away![546]

*

You can criticise anything. You can find good and bad in many things. To me, The Monkees were nothing but happiness and fun and silliness and youth.[547]

*

As a group, the Monkees were very, very popular. We went to 56 episodes, and we were in 36 countries around the world. The Monkees sold 75 million records. I believe good things stand the test of time.[548]

*

I believe thirty years from now [1996] they'll still be showing *The Monkees*, as they did *The Marx Brothers* and *The Dead End Kids* and *The Bowery Boys* and *The Three Stooges* and I'm not joking; I really think they will be.[549]

*

Micky and I and Peter, we've been pals for years and years and years, and we take care of each other.[550]

*

If anyone says anything about these guys, they'd better have their fists up. Because I have tremendous respect for them.

I might be putting them down and making fun of them, but *you* can't.[551]

*

We were thrown into something bigger than any of us could handle. But at the end of the day, we were brothers.[552]

*

We have all gotten closer. We're 20 years older now and have been through a lot. It's like we're all grown up now. We have all found each other, and for the first time we have so much in common. If anything we are more like brothers every day.[553]

*

I hope that *The Monkees* are remembered for the fun, and for the happiness that I think they showed, and the enjoyment that was obvious within the concept of their TV show.

It was just a fun time in my life, and I hope that will be what it was for a lot of people that shared that time with us, as mostly viewers.

It was one of the greatest experiences I've ever had and I'm sure that it will be remembered for the fun that it brought people.[554]

*

THE MONKEES
HOLLYWOOD WALK OF FAME
Presented To
The Monkees
on the occasion of the placement of your star in the
Hollywood Walk of Fame
July 10, 1989
HOLLYWOOD CHAMBER OF COMMERCE
BILL WELSH
PRESIDENT
JOHNNY GRANT
CHAIRMAN, WALK OF FAME

Talk About Music

My influences were my parents. I grew up (or didn't grow up as the case may be) in a musical-ish family. My mother played the piano. She played for the Christmas Nativity at the church, and my sisters ran the Youth Club, (and I was in the Boy Scouts — I can't tell you why I got thrown out, that's another story). But my dad used to sing to my mother all these songs that I didn't really understand at the time.

And she used to say, "Oh, shut up, Harry."[555]

*

The first record I ever bought was *Poetry in Motion* by Johnny Tillotson; I didn't even have a record player and I bought it. I was about twelve years old, and I used to sing songs like "Donna" by Ritchie Valens, and songs by Buddy Holly, with my mate, in hospitals and old folks homes.

They'd ask,"What about the little guy who sings those Buddy Holly songs?"

In between Elvis and The Beatles, there were all these pretty boys with the ties and the slicked back hair — teenage idols like Fabian, Frankie Avalon, and Bobby Rydell — those were my influences.[556]

*

Annabel Jones, pick her up. She's at Lady and the Lost Boys on Myspace or Google or whatever it is. She's an *amazing* little song writer, great little singer, and hopefully she'll see the light and come over to America and thrill and delight the audiences here, too.[557]

*

I have a lovely daughter who is a singer, Annabel Jones (Lady and the Lost Boys), is a great little singer and songwriter, but she's not at all ambitious, and I think that's why I survived in spite of myself.[558]

*

I love country music.

I wrote a song — I was watching *Nashville Now* a couple years back and I heard one of the country artists say that there's too many outsiders singing music. It's probably about ten years. Tommy Boyce and I sat down and we wrote a song called, "You Don't Have to Be a Country Boy to Write a Country Song."

I think music belongs to *everybody*. I know there are true country artists — people like Hank Williams and George Jones and Johnny Cash and Merle Haggard — but there are other people that have come into country, and there's a thing happening right now, young country, a crossover where it's got a little bit more rock into it. I'm not saying that it's as good as, it's just different.

And music is a thing that will change and change forever and ever, and nobody knows where it's going to go.

But you know, music does one thing: *it mingles souls*. And this is a very important thing. Because unless you listen to music — you must listen to music throughout the day — there are people that never talk to anybody throughout a day, there are people that don't listen to music. I have to do all that throughout my day: I have to talk to somebody, I have to shake somebody's hand or get a hug, and I have to listen to some music, and if that's my day, that's perfect.[559]

*

I've got an amazing band, some of them have been with me over 25 years. My joy is live performing. David Cassidy better be bloody good, if he's following us. Usually in my show I say, "If you like it, tell your friends, and if you didn't like it, tell 'em you saw David Cassidy." That's what I normally say, so I'll have to change that line to Micky Dolenz or something.[560]

*

When they asked me what I used to think my musical direction was, I always said Broadway Rock: a little bit of theatre, a little bit of rock and roll, which is more or less what happens in the seventies with people like Bowie and Alice Cooper and other theatrical presentations. So I was on the right track, just no one heard me.[561]

*

To share and collaborate with people — you can be a songwriter who writes on his own, but once you start collaborating and writing with other people it brings a different element into your life, and into your songs, somebody else's experiences, and therefore you're going onto a different thing. Whereas, as an individual, you're having your own experiences and then relating them through your music, through your art form or whatever it might be. Collaborating is something very special to me.[562]

*

There are more feelings and emotions than there are words to express them. And we should do it through the music.[563]

Talk About Peter Tork

They [the producers] were also interested in a couple of guys who turned the show down. One was Jerry Yester (he was with The Modern Folk Quintet, and now is the new addition to The Lovin' Spoonful), and Steve Sills of The Buffalo Springfield.

They liked Steve very much but he turned it down. He said, "That's not my bag, it's not what I want to do. But I do have a buddy — a friend of mine who's working out at Santa Monica in a coffee shop washing dishes; he plays guitar for his food."

So, Peter came down in blue jeans that were really dirty, his hair all over the place and un-shaven. Then Bert really flipped for Peter because of something he did. Peter went to sit down and [Bert] pulled the chair out from under him. So Peter calmly walked over and pulled all the things off the desk.

Then [Peter] said as if nothing had happened, "Do you want to get started now?" or something like that.[564]

*

Peter was Hare Krishna, waterbeds, brown rice, love, peace. Well, we *all* were really, but you know, that was the times.[565]

*

Peter was in another world: water beds, brown rice, Hare Krishna. He was scary. I didn't want to go to his house. I thought I'd be into some sort of orgy or some kind of drug den. I was kind of naive to all that stuff. Even Tommy Boyce and Bobby Hart, the songwriters, scared the pants off me.[566]

*

Peter and I hung out a couple of times, but it kind of scared me! Peter kind of scared me in a way because he was into the Hare Krishna, waterbeds, brown rice. I thought that meant going to India and becoming a Buddhist monk. I didn't really get it.

I thought, "Oh, pretty soon I'll be on the brown rice, and the waterbeds."

I hung out with him a few times to the point where I was over his house and there's Jim Morrison swimming in the pool with a bottle of whiskey in his hand, and different celebrities and people.[567]

*

Peace, love, waterbeds, Hare Krishna, brown rice — what about the seven stitches I had to have in my eye?

We settled that one with a little bit more aggression, but we won't go there.[568]

*

Peter decked me once. I had seven stitches put in my eye. I came back and gave him the bill. That's when it only cost $75 to have that done.[569]

*

Yeah, Peter and I, we had some fisty-cuffs at one point, but we were like brothers, and so you know, your brother steals your glory, or whatever it might be, you get a little… *uppity*!

We got a little pushy, and I gave him the Manchester Kiss, which is the forehead on the nose — *Bang*! — and he clocked me one.

We had to had stop the filming while I went to the hospital to get six stitches or something like that. But, you know, it was all for show really. I mean we couldn't go out on the street and start scuffling with somebody over nothing or whatever so we just picked on the closest person there was.[570]

*

We all did have little roles that we played, but Peter Tork was certainly *not* "the dummy". He was very intelligent. Very accomplished musician.[571]

*

I never really enjoyed the studio that much, but the fun thing about it was to see Peter, who, as I say, is a great musician, piano player, guitar player, drummer. He plays so many instruments, and very well too.[572]

*

Peter Tork plays seven or eight different instruments. And I mean, all at once, which is a problem but what can you do. In fact, he just joined a one man band but he gave it up because of musical differences.[573]

*

Peter is a musician that sings with Shoe Suede Blues. And if you talk to Peter, or any of these artists that were there [in the sixties], they are not living in the past. They are just taking advantage of the things that made them successful.[574]

*

This is true for the course with Peter. He always wanted to play in a band. And then when he *was* playing in a band [with The Monkees], he *still* wanted to play in a band. It's quite amazing, isn't it? I think with Peter, everything he tried to do, no matter *what* he tried to do, he was never *satisfied* at the end of it, and I think it was the closure at the end of it.[575]

*

I think in the beginning with Peter, it was all strange to him. So the music was his salvation, it was his comfort.[576]

*

I don't think we ever criticized each other. We always helped each other. Peter was very, *very* helpful to me. He always complimented me on my technique as far as music, and being able to relate to it, and keeping the beat, and keeping the perfect pitch and all things like that — but that was from my years of schooling on the stage.[577]

*

Peter Tork, gotta be the best musician in the band. He played guitar, bass, drums. He played some wind instruments. On the right material, he was really like the Ringo of the band, as far as the vocals were concerned, but very talented. Very, very talented musician. And as I say, always supportive. He bought me my first guitar. I've written over two hundred songs… and that was just this morning.[578]

*

Now Peter will never sing this song ["Hey, Hey, We're the Monkees"]; he hates it. I don't know why. This was our theme song. Not everybody has a theme song. I mean, this is the key. This is an identifiable thing. It's identification.[579]

*

Peter's soul left us about two and a half years ago.

He was a banjo player from Greenwich Village who was made into an actor and finally decided that he didn't want to be a Marx Brother forever.

His heart was back in the Village, that's all.[580]

Talk About Politics

I believe in Bobby Kennedy, and I believed in JFK, and in Martin Luther King, but they're all gone. And you know, it's either go along with it and try and do something about it, or just pull the trigger on yourself! It's really a weird, weird world.[581]

*

I think everybody's been put underneath the thumb, and there's too many people giving the orders: the people that have already got what they want out of life. What [the people in power] don't realize — and what they're *scared* of — they know what the young people are thinking, and in 25 years from now the people that they're knocking around are going to be running the world! I won't be because I, maybe, don't have it up here to be a great leader or something, but maybe my niece or something will be in government, in parliament, or something. Those are the people going to run the country, so [the people in power] better start treating them good now, or else they're going to be in trouble in 25 years from now.

We're going to be running the country in 25 years from now so you better be nice to us![582]

*

You work all your life, and you work for 14 pounds a week, 20 quid a week, and then you're allowed to take 50 pounds out of the country! Out of your *own* money! The money you've *earned*, the money you've *sweated* for! It doesn't seem right to me.

England at the moment is turning into little Russia. We say about the communist countries, we're being governed... We're turning into a little Russia, that's the only thing I can say. I don't think I *should* say that, I love England, and one day, that's where I'm going to die, in England. But I think we're being over governed.[583]

*

Kids in England, or America, or anyplace in the world, always do the *bang bang*, and the cowboy bit, and that's okay. But I think they take it for *real* in America. Well a lot of countries take it for real with the *bang bangs*.

But guns and killing? That's for the birds. Forget that. Because it doesn't work.[584]

*

We have a new lease on the country with politicians giving their time and their energy. *Yes we can!* What a great saying: Yes we can! Ask not what your country can do for you, but what you can do for your country. Obama... (I make jokes about everything, I love comedy, I love theatre, and I do shtick and I get away with it because I like it. I don't want to be Jay Leno or Conan O'Brien, or that kind of presentation reading from a script, but I was trying to think of something funny about Obama...)

What has Obama, Peter Tork, and Prince Charles got in common?

They're the only three people I know that can whisper in their own ears!

He's got these big ears, but he's a beautiful looking man, and he's very articulate.[585]

Talk About Possessions

This ring I gave myself [is my prized material possession]. It is white gold with a black star sapphire and diamonds in it. It symbolizes many things to me.[586]

*

In almost every room there is at least one of my hand paintings. I don't paint hands simply for my own sake — I just love collecting really good and lifelike paintings of hands. It's funny the things that appeal to people, isn't it? I mean to say, take a foot. Who'd want a picture of a foot?[587]

*

In my garage these days [1968], you will find a brand new Honda car. Yes, it is made by the very same people who make Honda motorbikes. It is British racing green, has its own hi-fi stereo inside — and it's a "gem".[588]

*

My favorite room is the garage. My garage is not like anybody else's. You see, I have had it converted into a soundproof studio where I go to compose, play the guitar and listen to playbacks of the material I have done.

While I was in England, I ordered a big new pool table. When it gets here, I am going to put that in the garage. My English Honda car, in British racing blue, was also waiting for me when I returned — complete with hi-fi radio-stereo! I love it, but I also dig riding around on my Triumph motorcycle. Just call me "Wheels" Jones![589]

*

And I still have the bass! I have the *original* bass. I think there was only a couple of them made too. It's a shorter bass than the basses they have, you know. Which I think would be a good thing to have that right now, actually.[590]

*

The family dog's name is Dodger. He's called Dodger because I played the Artful Dodger in *Oliver!* My dad registered him at the Kennel Club as the "Artful Dodger" and we call him Dodger for short.[591]

*

I have a brand new friend living with me. Don't get nervous — it's just Susie, my new German shepherd pup. Susie, the gift of a fan, is black, and is about five months old. Susie is a *he*, but I named him Susie in memory of my first dog — which was stolen.[592]

*

Getting to things more domestic, I thought you might like to know that my dog Susie managed to chew a great big hole in the wooden fence around my house. I guess Susie (who is a he, not a she) doesn't dig being fenced in! Unfortunately, I have to have a fence or else some of my ever-luvvin' fans might get onto my property. The last time I was "invaded," someone released the brake on one of my cars and caused it to crash.[593]

*

I have an apartment in Santa Barbara, California. In fact, in Manteca, where Peter is, but mine's at the Polo Fields. I've had that for a number of years. I have a home in Pennsylvania; I bought it in '87, I was writing my first book, *They Made a Monkee Out of Me*, and a guy I knew lived there. I went there, I saw the house — big old three-story yellow house with sun porches, 16 acres of land at the back. I've put in an all-weather racetrack around the outside, and my dream has been the Maryland Cup. Whether I'll stay there after *this* winter is another story all together![594]

*

When I walked in the door I knew this was my house. If not now, at some point. Three, five, seven days after I came back [after buying the house], there's my neighbour walking in my yard holding up two dead squirrels.

I said, "Hey, I've got kids, you know, you can't do that.'

[Davy then outlawed hunting on his 16 acres.][595]

*

I don't worry about security [at the Beavertown house], I worry about which leak will spring next.[596]

*

Oh, I've got ghosts out the yin yang. A lot of their stuff is still in the drawers. Baking utensils. Social Security cards.[597]

*

I just bought a church, we raised the steeple over the weekend, and the weathercock went on there, which was a horse, and the bell was in, and I'm going to make myself a soundstage and rehearsal studio out of this beautiful old building, this Lutheran church, which was more or less falling down, which we have now lifted from the wreckers, they were going to come in. It's beautiful wooden beams, and beautiful high ceilings. Maybe Davy Jones pictures. It's definitely going to be a memorabilia museum, and also a rehearsal studio. We've got a 64 track digital recording studio down the road, and so we're well equipped in a very little town. And the amish carriages go by, and the people are up there working, I'm working amongst the people that are working, and that's the way I like it.[598]

*

My town, called "Beavertown", Pennsylvania, (I liked the name so I bought the place!) I have a nice home there, and I also own a church, which I've converted into a memorabilia museum, and a children's theatre. So that's something I've worked on for a number of years, and that's going to come to fruition by next spring and into the summer and hopefully the first production will be taking place, and the memorabilia museum will be opening, and I've got stuff from many many different artists, and Monkees, and other collectors in the neighbourhood. My neighbour has got a collection as big as this room with all antique cars, and little first edition cars, and that would nice to say: "Jim Straub Car Collection", and maybe next month have some paintings from Graham Nash, or guitars.

But, build it and they will come!

Be safe, buy local![599]

Talk About Prejudice

I hate to see the kids [on Sunset Strip] getting a tough deal just because they are kids and have long hair. And that kind of prejudice is just as immoral as any other and it does exist.[600]

*

I look better with my hair short. My father doesn't like long hair. Without long hair I wouldn't have this job. So I say people should take us for what we *are*.

Not for what's on the *outside* of the head, but what's *in* the head.[601]

*

There's a kind of mutual misunderstanding. Somehow being a teenager in the U.S. is a long term thing because young people stay on longer at college. In England I was out earning a living for myself at sixteen and had left school — expected to be treated as an adult. In some states you're lucky if they treat you as a human being if you have long hair and are riding a motor-bike. And don't get the idea that all Americans are intolerant — I've got some good friends out there. The U.S. has been good to me and I'm grateful. But you can get brought down by the mentality which thinks you're a moron if your hair is over your collar.[602]

*

ell of course [this hospitality I foresee in three years is going to include colored people]. It used to be that way.

I understand that there's hundreds of people, thousands of people in England that are out of work, and my dad would say, "I've got my mate here at work, and he's not working anymore, and we've got these Pakistanis coming over here and doing this and taking *our* jobs!"

And I said, "Dad, don't look at it like that; if the Pakistani guy is the guy that can do the job *better* than the guy from England, give *him* the job!"

Everything is competition. And if your competition is better than you are, step aside and let them do it. I'm not saying the blacks or the whites or the pinks or the greens are better than anybody, it's just that everybody should have an *even break*. It doesn't matter who was here first, whether the blacks or the whites were here first. It doesn't matter whether Jesus had woolly hair like a negro would have, or he had long hair, it doesn't matter!

And that makes me laugh, too: they made a big stink about people with long hair. In America I get people laughing because of my hair, and George Washington had long hair, Benjamin Franklin, Jesus was supposed to have long hair — the negroes would say that Jesus had wooly type hair. Everything used to be so *informal*, and it's not anymore. It's so formal. Everybody's so *tense*, it's like somebody's got hold of everybody's backbone and *pulled* them. Everybody's on the guard the whole time. I know *I* am.[603]

*

There are three things you are supposed to steer clear of in an interview: religion, politics and sex.

See my badge? [*Jewish Power*] I'm sending away for another one which reads: *Sterilise LBJ — No more ugly children.*604

*

Within the coming years [1968], England's gotta join the common market and they've got to start mixing. We used to be fantastic mixers — anybody could come to this country because they knew they could mix; whether you're black, pink, blue, orange, it doesn't matter what colour you are, they'd come here because they knew England is noted for hospitality, but not anymore.605

*

We are just reviewing a song right now, and don't be offended, please, I thought about [how] we're becoming much more liberal, and very democratic towards our conversation, and not being so uptight, where we used to *not* be.

Chris Rock, he's always talking about white boys. And you've got Latin comedians talking about black people. White people are so *afraid* of taking about *anybody*. So there was this one song back in the sixties called "Melting Pot", and it says: "Take a piece of white man, wrap him up in black skin, add a touch of blue blood, and a little bit of Red Indian, too." It says, "Curly, black and kinkies, mixed with yellow chinkies. Put them all together and we got a recipe for a get along scene. I better call out the Queen, it's only fair she knows, you know, because what we need is a great big melting pot. Take the world and all it's got. Keep it turning for a hundred years or more, and turn out coffee coloured people by the score."

What we need is a great big melting pot, and that's what we're getting. I think the world has got so much potential right now, and there's all kinds of opinions about religion and the way forth. My bible is John Lennon's songs. My bible is "music mingles souls". We've never had a war over music! You get people that don't even listen to the radio throughout the day. When people complain about this kind of music, or that kind of music, or what do you think about rap music, what do you think about this (I mean, I say tongue-in-cheek: rap music — they missed a C off the front), but you wouldn't imagine Bobby Rydell going after Fabian because he has a hit record! Shooting him in the knees![606]

*

And look what's happened in the world today, thirty-five years ago they had front doors for whites and back doors for blacks. I was in Makin, Georgia, the other day, and it said on the sign outside the factory: *Coloured/Whites*. And there's a proposition to take it down. Don't take it down! Leave that as history. It doesn't happen anymore, we're over all that kind of stuff. You don't see little kids seeing prejudice in people.[607]

Talk About Purpose

My father always said, "Find out what you do best, and do it."[608]

*

All I want to do is: I want to perform, I want to entertain as long as I can. I love entertaining. I look forward to that intimate situation so that people can see me, up front, and see me instead of having to read about what I've done. That's why I keep performing in between all the things that I do otherwise.[609]

*

It's about having a good time and enjoying what you're doing. The performance is the most important thing to me. That's when I'm the most clearest to myself, and I enjoy myself when I get on the stage and I start to perform.[610]

*

When I get in front of the camera, or I'm on the stage, that's when I do what I do. Some guys are a carpenter or a plumber, or whatever he might do, he *shines* when he does that particular thing. When I leave here, I'm not "Davy Jones" with the stars in his eyes, telling jokes, and messing around all the time, I'm not that kind of an entertainer. I do go onto a stage and I like to improvise and if somebody says a word, I can pick up on it and I can take it on from there, and I enjoy doing that. I'm not afraid of making mistakes. If anything, as an entertainer, I'm rather *not* very ambitious, and I think maybe if I *was*, then I would be in Hollywood doing a situation comedy, or looking for that part in that movie, or looking for a new recording contract. I'm quite happy doing what I do. I get a lot of yeses, you know. It's not necessarily Oscar time, and grammy awards and everything else, but it *could* be; it's the amount of time you put in, or how much you want it, and I'm quite satisfied with what I do.[611]

*

You want to find out from the people how much you can really do. I know *what* I am; I don't really know *where* I want to go. I know what I'm going to do to get there: I'm going to play it straight all the way and I'm only going to give as much as they want me to give.[612]

*

I'm not locked in to any one thing: I've written a couple of books, I work in the theatre, I work in television — I don't do that much television, I'm not a big fan of situation comedy. The Monkees was great and we made 56 episodes, it went to 36 countries around the world, we sold a hundred million records. Top that! So I don't really go looking for another TV series. But theatre, working here [Merv Griffin's Resort, Atlantic City], doing a show that's live, to me, is my most favourite time, and I am sort of an up front forward person in that sense, and my relief is definitely the live audience, the theatre. Other than that, I'm sort of lost, I'm wandering helpless.[613]

*

I'm looking for answers, and I found it through my work, and through my traveling, and that's the fortunate thing about it. I've been able to go all over the world.[614]

*

My kids give me motivational speaking. My daughter told me the other day, when I call up sometimes she puts the phone down and walks around and does stuff because I go on a lot. Because I'm talking about horses, I'm talking about this, I'm talking about that, but only to find my *own* answers! I'm not doing it to impress anybody with my knowledge of anything. This is why I continue to travel and work and perform, it's because I have answers to find as well. I can't do it sitting at home.[615]

*

I write songs, but not because I have aspirations that have them going to the charts. I have lots of albums that I've made, and written lots of tunes. It's just an expression of my poetry that I put to music. I'm not a great guitar player, but I love to play, and I sit and I write, and it's just an exercise, an instrument.

Don't tell me you *used* to be a drummer; don't tell me you *used* to play the bass; or *used* to play the guitar. You *do*. And *do* it. Break away for a moment. Get out of the schedule, the ritual of mowing the lawn on a Saturday — you don't do it in the winter, so what do you do with *that* time? Go up into the attic. Get your instrument out. Start strumming. Or start playing your drums, or doing whatever you're doing.[616]

*

Someone said to me, "I used to be a drummer".

I said, "No, you didn't *used* to be a drummer. You *are* a drummer, and you need get back on the drums and just play.[617]

*

There are so many great song writers in this country, in America, and around the world, and so many great writers that write books, and so many great artists that paint, that will never ever be heard or seen, but it doesn't mean that you're not on the best-seller list, and it doesn't mean that you're not on the top of the charts, and it doesn't mean that, because you're not on the top of the bill that you're not any good. Because if you stop at a holiday inn, or you stop at another restaurant, or you stop at a club and you listen to bands and musicians playing, you say to yourself, "I might as well quit now," because some of them are so fantastic and so good. But it's being at the right place at the right time. I was lucky and I love to entertain, and that's what I do — I'm not a singer/songwriter, a dancer, actor, but I love to *entertain*. To me it's absolutely no different than the school play, and I get paid for this now, and I'll continue to do it as long as I feel that I enjoy it.[618]

*

Writing is something that doesn't always have to be at the top of the charts to be a great song. It doesn't have to be always a bestseller to be a great book. So those people out there with a flair for any one of these two professions, just keep doing it! Cos nobody does what you do. So just keep doing it.[619]

*

If I don't like something, no matter what it is — I don't care whether there's money involved or even if there's feelings involved, which is very hard — if I don't *like* it and I don't feel it's *right*, if I have to think twice about something, I won't do it.

You got to be 100% sure. If you say to yourself, "I'm going to do this, I think I'll go on my own... yeah, but maybe I won't..."

If I ever think that [uncertain], that's the end of the line for me.[620]

*

It's attitude. It's attitude. If you want to have longevity, you've got to have the attitude and desire. It doesn't matter whether you're playing at the Holiday Inn, or you're playing at the

Ritz. As long as you feel *good* about what you do, that's who you are.

I don't care what anyone says about my performance or whether I'm good, bad or indifferent. I'm who I am and I can't change that.[621]

*

If there was any advice I could give to anybody about show business (and any advice anyone can give *me* please give me a call!) but the thing is, my dad told me: nobody does what you do. You're an individual, you're unique.

And so, for all those kids and adults that are going up for auditions, and meeting people, and being tested all the time — there's nothing worse than being tested and *not* being chosen. That's really hard because you obviously take it personally. Even when they did the Godfather, Al Pacino and the other people in there, they had to audition. But it's always a *test*, and it's always something that is kind of scary in a way, because, "Wait a minute… I *know* how to act; I'm an actor! I can do *anything*. Why do I have to *test* to be able to display my art, and show people what I can do?"

Never give up.

Nobody does what you do.

Just believe in yourself and focus on what you want to do.

There's a word that has helped me, and it's something you've got to believe in; it's called *empowerment*. You've got to take hold of this and say: "I *can* do it. I know eventually somebody else is gonna realize that I can, too."

So don't give up.

Keep knocking on the doors because the door to opportunity is marked *push*.

Just don't stop wanting.

Never give up your dream.

Everyone's always said it, and I'm never gonna give up my dream; I want to keep doing it 'til I make it.[622]

Talk About Religion

Sunday was a very special day for our family. My mother was very religious, a very, very soulful person, and she always liked us to go to church.[623]

*

One of my early recollections is of going to church, which my family always did. I hated it, because I had to sit still, and I'm definitely not one who sits still! I wanted to join the church choir very much, but every time I would sing, everyone would tell me I had a terrible voice, so I never got in. Fancy that!

*

We're all going to end up in the same place; we're all going to be ending up on our backs, in the end, so it doesn't matter. We're put on the world for *some* reason, I don't know what it is.

When somebody says, "Do you believe in God?" I believe in God because my father's told me; I don't really know myself.

I *do*, not because it's the "in" thing to do, I believe in God because you got to believe in something.[624]

*

Young people have become bored and confused by the established Church. There are so many conflicting dogmas and religions all claiming that they are right and the other is wrong. Someone should make them put their heads together and come up with a new religion acceptable to all.

How can one small section of the community claim to be all right and that the others are all wrong? I'm not an irreligious person — I read the Bible frequently, and it contains much truth and beauty. My mother read it to me a lot when I was a child.[625]

*

You could take [the song "It's Not Too Late"] as a gospel message.

There are many ships in life heading the wrong way. They could all be turned around, and put right, with forgiveness and love.[626]

*

I tend to try to do unto others as they do unto me, you know, and be a good Christian.[627]

*

A priest had told his congregation that (before passing on) you must go off to a monastery, or to a retreat, or someplace, for three or four days to prepare to go to wherever you're going to go when you go.

The first thing they do when you get there is tell you how much you sinned, whether you have or not.

So I thought about it, and I just realized that *this* is my monastery. This is my retreat. The *stage*! So, I come up and get myself prepared, for tomorrow, the next day, next week, or whatever it might be.

And *this* is my retreat![628]

*

Davy Jones family bibles sold at auction in 2015

Talk About Sex

I never slept with [Gloria Stavers, 16 Magazine editor]. Most of the stars did to get on the front, but I didn't.[629]

*

There weren't that many girls around because all our fans were quite young, you know. There wasn't backstage parties where everybody got crazy. We were so busy traveling and working. It was very little time to do anything other than The Monkees for about two years straight. Three years straight.[630]

*

There were groupies, but not that many. Our fans were mostly aged between nine and 14. And even if there were women, we were so guarded by security that we couldn't do anything about it. The pop star David Cassidy was picked up so many times he started to grow handles. But I wasn't promiscuous… not that my wife believes me.[631]

*

My band member called me up the other day and he says, "I want to ask you a question: Do you think it's kinda weird that when I have sex, when I make love, I leave my socks on?"

I said, "Eric, it's your house, it's your computer, you can do anything you want!"[632]

*

My bandmate went to the doctors, and the doctor said, "Eric, you've got to stop masturbating."

He said, "Why?"

The doctor said, "Because I won't be able to examine you if you don't."[633]

*

What's the difference between pink and purple?

The grip.[634]

*

There were all kinds of stuff that went on. You know I had an experience. We came into this hotel and we were staying there. And it was late at night, and I was with one of the boys — who shall be nameless because he's asked me *never* to tell who it was.

We met these two girls, and we were having a little "lemonade" at the bar there. And we had a little dance with them. And we were well in touch here!

I was having a little dance with this rather large girl and she gave me a kiss, and then I realized that her Adam's apple was bigger than mine!

So I left, posthaste! And ran! I said [to the person who shall remain nameless], "I'm going to bed, I'll see you tomorrow."

And he said, "No, no don't leave! Don't leave me, this is gonna be a sure thing! Don't go!"

I said, "I am going to bed." I made a comment about what I thought he would be finding later on in the evening — I'd kissed this guy, right, and I went… that's a *guy*! And so I went over to my partner and said, "I've only got one thing to say to you before I go… I've only got one thing to say to you, and that's all I'm gonna say… Dick and balls."

And then I left.

So, off he went to his room, and I understand he spent the rest of the night locked in the bathroom because he found out more information than he needed!

I don't know how he didn't know, but he got in bed with this guy, and then realized what was going on, and jumps up, got in the bathroom and locked the door!

He never forgave me for that. He was white the next day. He didn't speak to me for two weeks. Sorry, Micky, I had to tell them.[635]

*

I can honestly tell you that during The Monkees '67-'68 tour, I might've got laid twice, with people that sort of casually came by, and we were on the road for a long time. It was always the crew that got laid, not the guys. As far as groupies, I never saw any of them. There was no wild sex orgy at my house.

In 1976, there were a lot of women in my life and in my bed, and I enjoyed it. It was something I missed out on, coming from England at 15 and getting into theatre. I mean, I don't think I had my first sex until I was 17 or 18. I lived a very quiet life and was very inactive in that particular department. In '76, it was as if I'd just found a new toy. I must say I used it as often as possible. Groupies to me, were people who followed you around. Familiar faces who were always there, asking for autographs. We have more of those now, but they're not sexual. I don't fancy any of it. I'm a married man. If I want sex at this particular point in my life, I go home for it.[636]

*

(Do you like women with big breasts?)

I like all women, I've never met a girl yet that I didn't like, but it all depends, I'd have to see the rest of the product too.

(But a nice set doesn't hurt?)

A nice set doesn't hurt. Unless it falls on you from a great height.

(During foreplay, what percentage of the time do you spend on breasts?)

A major, major part of the time I would spend on breasts. Just on one breast.

(How many minutes? When you make love to a woman does it take an hour?)

Who can last five minutes these days! I would definitely spend a major, major time on the breast before I work my way into other parts of the anatomy.

(Now that you're older, do you have to put up with sagging breasts, like so many older men?)

I have a wife. She's very attractive.

(But she's older now, right?)

She is older, yes. She doesn't have sagging breasts…

(But you anticipate having to put up with that at some point?)

Well, if that's what happens with all women's breasts, yes, I'll have to "put up with it".

(Were you breast fed?)

I was breast fed, and I'm still being breast fed, actually.

(Does your wife have beautiful breasts? Is she a C cup?)

She has very, very nice breasts, and she's not a very big girl, I would say somewhere in the middle there.

Yes [I'm putting out an album], I'm putting it out the door cos it's terrible! I'm always working on something, but all I've got on my mind right now are *breasts!*[637]

*

I sat next to this lady on the aeroplane, and it was quite cute 'cause I have a bit of a way sometimes.

I said, "Where are you going?"

She said, "I'm going to New York City."

I said, "That's funny, so am I. What do you do?"

She said, "I travel all over the world — different towns, different cities — to find out who are the best lovers."

I went, "Whoa, that's nice. So who *are* the best lovers?"

She said, "American Indians, and Jewish guys."

I said, "Very nice. I'm very pleased to meet you, my name is Tonto Eisenberg."[638]

*

In the old days I was picked up so much I got handles. Now… I sat alone next to the fire on New Years Eve and strummed a guitar.[639]

Talk About The Sixties

1964 that was the first TV show I did, *The Ed Sullivan Show*, the same night The Beatles were on. Which put me into that mode of: "Hey… Look at all these girls!" I watched them sing six tunes, and I thought: "My goodness gracious. Well, I'm from England, I think I could do that!"[640]

*

I just watched what [The Beatles] were doing from behind the curtain [on *The Ed Sullivan Show*] and I thought, "I want to do this. Look at all those girls!" And here I thought you couldn't get any bigger or better than the standing ovations we were getting in *Oliver!*[641]

*

It was interesting [being on *Ed Sullivan* the same night as The Beatles]. During *Oliver!* we had occasion to go on the show. I was standing in the elevator and Ringo Starr got in. He's obviously a nice chap and he's got his qualities, but he was an ugly bugger, you know. He had this massive nose. Pop singers were sort of like Dave Clark and Paul McCartney. I always tell a joke about Ringo. I said I met him in the elevator, he had a bad cold at the time, and he was just about to blow his nose and I said, "No, let me hold the handkerchief. I'm closer than you are." He had to make two turns around the corner, it seemed to me.

And then I saw what happened on the show, and I couldn't believe it. And that's when it first struck me. Within two, three weeks, I was signed to Colpix Records and I was in the studio making some demos.[642]

*

You know, the first band with a manufactured image wasn't The Monkees. It was The Beatles. Brian Epstein (their manager) told them: look this way, move your head this way, move your hair this way. This is how you've got to play the game.[643]

*

That was one of the biggest compliments when we were doing the show, that people sort of likened us to The Beatles. Obviously, in our heads, it was kind of a bit bizarre, but we really tried anyway. We tried to simulate a bit of what they were doing, the fun that they used to put into their music and appearances more than anything.[644]

*

Against The Beatles? You must be joking. The Beatles are gods to us, man. I never said they were on their way out. All I said was that I thought they were *tired* — if I had had five years of the kind of work and exposure they've had I know *I'd* be tired. I'd never put a group like that down. Oh, listen, I've bought every album they've ever made, and when I was in New York I hitched all the way to San Francisco and spent all my money just to see them in concert. Now does that sound as if I'm anti-Beatles?[645]

*

The Beatles gave us a party. They gave us a great party in London. I'm told it's a great party; I didn't actually go. It was the one day I had off, and I went off to see my sister in Thetford, Norfolk[646]

*

I just read in a book that Eric Clapton, the first time he took LSD was with The Monkees. Well, I wasn't there. It was in London, and there was a meeting with The Beatles, and that night was the only night I could travel to go see my sisters. So I went to see my sisters, I didn't go to the occasion with The Beatles and Eric Clapton and Mick Jagger or whom else was there, Harry Nilsson and whatever. And I understood from this book that he took LSD with The Monkees. But *I* wasn't there, *I* didn't take LSD with Eric Clapton, but as far as anyone reading that book, Davy Jones did.[647]

*

I've met all The Beatles. Ringo would be somebody that I'd seen more often over the years than the other boys. I'd been to sessions where Paul was there with Linda. And George Harrison was a frequent visitor to Micky Dolenz's house — as was Marc Bolan, and Ringo, and Harry Nilson and lots of other people. You really take it in your stride. Obviously, I'm a big fan of the business.[648]

*

Hendrix was a regular kind of a guy. He launched "Foxy Lady" off our show, and all of a sudden he had a cult following — I think Woodstock and Monterey Pop also helped with that.

Micky saw him in a club in New York, and asked him, would he come on tour with us, he said, "Oh yeah, sure."

He didn't know who The Monkees were.[649]

*

Chaz Chandler was the manager [of The Jimi Hendrix Experience], and it was quite a coup for him to get Hendrix on the bill because it gave him national exposure. And I remember reading later that he'd said that it was the biggest mistake he ever made, but I think it was the best thing that happened to Hendrix because he was like a backup musician for like The Four Tops. They were cool guys. We used to hang out when we did the shows, toured all over the country, and he was quite a regular sort of chap. That left-handed guitar thing was new... I used to play left-handed trumpet![650]

*

Free love. I was once at Peter Tork's house, and the pool was *full* of people. Naked. Jim Morrison was at one end of the pub — uh, pool. Ha, yeah, "the pub". He'd been in the pub all night I think. I'm not sure. He had a bottle of something in his hand. And Barry McGuire, "The Eve of Destruction". Stephen Stills. Man, it was lots of times we hung out with lots and lots of people. It was more of a fun party for everybody.

We used to see The Association, or we'd see The Turtles, Mark and Howie, and more or less like: "'Ey, we'll knock you off the charts next week, mate."

It was not sort of run by the lawyers and businesspeople. I guess it was, but, you know, it seemed a little more freeform, I guess.[651]

*

It was unbelievable, really. My dad, he just took it in his stride, and he was very, very proud. So it was all very family. And I think that's a lot to do with the reasons I never really got into anything other than the normal sort of drug of choice at the time. Marijuana, we used to smoke. Kinda silly in a sense when you think about it, because everybody was kind of crazy and sixties and sort of Woodstock and Monterey Pop Festival. I had responsibilities to my family and friends that I'd known for years, so I was always a little worried about how they would feel. So that was always the thought I'd had in my mind when we started to over-party.[652]

*

When we did The Johnny Cash Show I established a friendship with him. I love Johnny Cash, he's a charming man.

He called me up once from Montego Bay. "This is Johnny Cash speaking."

I said, "Who is it really?"

"No, it's Johnny Cash."

I said, "Where are you?"

He said, "Montego Bay."

I said, "No, I know it's not Johnny Cash."

He said, "Well, my granddaughter loves you and I want you to come and see her."

And I said, "Well, I'll be in Nashville."

He said, "I know you're gonna be there, boy, I'm comin' to see you."

So we played Nashville and he came to see me and I went to his house and I've been there many times since, but he took me to his bedroom and Johnny and June have their own quarters, their own bathrooms — one for his and one for hers. It makes for a happy marriage. He took me to his bathroom, and I looked down and he's got a see-through toilet seat with barbed wire in it. He said, "That's how I wrote the song, boy: I fell into a burning ring of fire!"[653]

*

That's America. Well, that kind of thing, [political assassination] it'd never happen in England. I don't think we've had somebody, either in royalty or somebody in the government, assassinated, have we? Or if it has, it's been a long, long, long time ago. Something like that is, to me, typically, *American*, you know what I mean? You can't avoid it, I don't suppose, but it's something that I… Don't ask me about it right now because I just heard it, I just read it in the paper on the way down here. It's just unbelievable. It can't… You know it *can't* happen. But it… But it has.[654]

*

It's like what [Robert] Kennedy wants to do, he wants to let the people run it. I saw a thing on the news where he was at a college campus and they were shouting and screaming and everybody was excited because he's a young cat, he's 42 years old or something, and everybody had this *young* feeling, even the older people were really bouncing because they got somebody like his brother coming in. And he had the same thoughts and the same feelings, and all of a sudden, *bang!* I don't know what's gonna happen, I pray to God that he's gonna be okay.[655]

*

I think within the next three years there's going to be a lot of things happening in the world. I've felt this for like seven months, I keep turning around to my friends, saying, "Something's in the air! I don't know what it is, I don't know whether it's with *me*, or whether it's with *you*, or whether it's with *everybody*, but something's in the air. *Something's* going to happen."

And just like little things (*big* things) that have made so much difference to all our lives — like (John) Kennedy going, and Martin Luther King, and Bobby Kennedy getting shot, and things like that — when something like that happens, something *else* happens to cool it out.

Like when Martin Luther King got shot, the people of America didn't know that the biggest raids on North Vietnam were being made that day. They were bombed. They laid more bombs down on that country than ever was laid down before, and they didn't hear about that in the papers because all they heard was Martin Luther King.

Now somebody's *behind* all this. Somebody's making a lot of money out of war. 1968! We shouldn't have a war! We're all civilized people! We're walking around with coats and ties and nice things and good shoes and why do we need a war? The only reason we need a war is because somebody's making some money.

I think that in three years from now we're going to see Russia and America together; it's got to be. We're going to see England, they're going to start giving like they used to, people are going to want to come here. If I ever have any children they're going to be born here because I want that English passport, because I'm proud of that; everybody in the world wants an English passport. They want to come because you're free! It's not that way now, but in three years from now we're going to be in the common market; we're going to be cooled out; we're going to get somebody come along that's got *young* ideas, like Bobby Kennedy, and we're all going to have to keep him safe. We're all going to have to get round him and make sure that he makes it, because he's gonna help us. You're gonna help the people. We might be all doing well now — we all might be doing well with the money, and we're all having a good time, we're eating good meals — but you know in three years from now, we might *not* be. And these people that are laying down the laws are going to want *more*. They're always going to want more, because *I* want more! I know what they want because they're laying down these laws that I don't really agree with, but I have to go along with them because if I don't, I might get shot![656]

*

All the kids want, really, not something to look up to, or something to copy, they want something that they can look at and just get it out of their system.

When they scream, they're not screaming because, "Oh, Davy!" or "Mike!" or "Paul!" or "John!", it doesn't matter, they don't scream because they see a *face*, they scream, really, because they want to get it *out!* Everybody's trying to get something *out* of themselves — whether it's going and have a drink in the pub, and playing a piano and singing, or having a smoke, or marijuana, or whatever it is — everybody's trying to get something *out* that's never been out before!

Everybody knows when they reach it in life, when it really comes out, and they really feel as if they've bloomed, and they feel on top of the world. I'm sure one day I'll look back on this [talking to you], and it'll seem a long way away.[657]

*

When we did the TV show, we met lots of celebrities, obviously. You know, there were fans. Paul McCartney sent a letter saying, "Could you send an autographed picture and a record to my daughter." Who now is, I think, works for *Chanel* or something in Paris, as a designer. So there was lots of contact from lots of people, and in fact there's lots of fans that were celebrities. You know, I've met Sylvester Stallone: "Hey, Davy, how you doin', I'm a big fan of The Monkees, you know, hey!" (Then give us a job, mate, in your next movie!)

Jack Nicholson was doing spaghetti westerns like Clint Eastwood, and he was doing small parts. I think he showed up on *Bewitched*, and shows like that. Jack Nicholson, in the early days. And then he was friends with Bert Schneider and Bob Rafelson, *The Monkees* producers, so he brought them in, and we did the movie called *Head*.[658]

*

Girls come to me and tell me they used to keep my picture on their bedroom wall, sort of kiss it good night. And they kissed the television when The Monkees were on, which was very dangerous in the 60's because we had those electrified carpets. I know because I got third-degree burns from watching *I Dream of Genie*, you know what I'm saying?[659]

*

There's lots of things in the sixties that we tend to forget. I love the music of the sixties. I love the bands, and the whole feel of the sixties, now that was when I had a lot of fun. I'm having great fun now [1990]![660]

Talk About Success

Booker T. Washington said, "Success is not to be measured by the position you reach in life, but by the obstacles you overcome to reach that success." [*I have learned that success is to be measured not so much by the position that one has reached in life as by the obstacles which he has overcome while trying to succeed.*][661]

*

It was a big deal for me as a 16 year old kid at the time to be nominated for a Tony Award! The awards are great, but more the *performance* and the *engagements* and the things that you *do* when you're making that step towards success.

"Success is not to be measured by the position you reach in life, it's the obstacles you overcome to reach that success".[662]

*

The reason [the cast of *Oliver!*] wanted to do *The Ed Sullivan Show* was because, supposedly, if you went on *The Ed Sullivan Show*, that *made* your career. But no one show *makes* your career. It's like the kids on *American Idol*, or the contestants on *Dancing With the Stars*, or what have you, it doesn't mean they're gonna get the Chita Rivera part in *West Side Story* just because they danced well. It doesn't mean they're gonna get a long career. It all depends on who you've got around you, who's supporting you, and how grounded you can become in regards to your success.[663]

*

I was never really overwhelmed by the success. It's all been the same to me. I always felt that this was my calling; this is what I *do*. So The Monkees was no bigger to me — honestly, I swear to you — than playing Tom Sawyer in the school play. And if I was to think any different, you know, show business is a minefield.[664]

*

Of course luck plays a big part when you're first starting out. You've got to be in the right place at the right time like I was. But it's a funny thing, if you work hard all the time, the luck always seems to happen, but if you don't work hard, then even if you get lucky it won't make any difference because you won't last. After you get rich, you don't need luck any more, but if you've worked as hard as you're supposed to you'll still continue to get it.[665]

*

When you've got success, everyone wants to know you. The times that I've been given and offered stuff, it's amazing, and then other times, when you need stuff, then nobody's there for you… so…

Success is… phew… it's got a little *trickery* to it.[666]

*

I was at Colonial Downs just outside of Richmond for a couple of seasons. I'm at the barn there, on my own, looking after some horses. And this one owner came to say thank you to his horse who had just won. He had a kid with him, and the kid was speaking Spanish, and I knew that he was talking about giving the horse some carrots. I had bags of them, waiting to feed mine later, so I went over and gave him half a dozen carrots. And the owner came down, shook my hand, and put a twenty dollar bill in it.

And he says, "Thank you very much."

And I said, "Hey, you're quite welcome."

That was the greatest moment of the whole time at Colonial Downs. Some guy gave me a twenty for giving his horse some carrots. He didn't know about Davy Jones from The Monkees. My hat was on, my hair was back, I was dirty from the day. Unknown and anonymous — that's the secret to success.[667]

*

When you become an entertainer and you become successful, you become "better looking", you become "more intelligent", you become this "wealthy" person that you not necessarily are. Or this grounded person, this authority, this source of information. But it's all kind of a falsehood and I think people take it too seriously, and that's what you've *not* got to do. Don't stop listening and learning, and I think that's the secret to success in the business.[668]

*

March 81   Sussex

Success is not to be measured
By the position you reach in life
But by the obstacles you overcome
to reach that success —
    Energy is Eternal Delight
            Daniel Jones

Talk About USA

I was 16 when I left for America and I was feeling so grown up! I'll never forget the trip over. I got on the plane with the show's choreographer who was around 30 years old. I was feeling so adult and the stewardess came round and asked what we wanted to drink. The choreographer ordered something like scotch and water and then the stewardess turned to me and said "And would your son like milk?" Oh, it was the biggest put down!

We arrived in Toronto. The *Oliver!* company had several weeks on the road before opening on Broadway. The boy I was replacing in the show had not even been told I was going to take over and we were supposed to open in two weeks in New York! So I was locked in my hotel room.

My first impressions are probably typical. I was surprised that everyone stared at my long hair. It wasn't that long, but nobody even looked twice in England. I was knocked out by the department stores. They seemed really, really big to me.

I loved steak and had it nearly every day for quite a while, because I'd never tasted it before. When we arrived in New York we stayed at the Royal York Hotel and it really impressed me. I'd never stayed in a hotel before. It's funny because now it seems like nothing to me.[669]

*

When I came to New York and lived on my own, I remembered the feeling, and I remembered looking up at these big, tall buildings, and walking: *Don't walk, Walk, Cross*. Don't worry. "What is all this? It's amazing!"

They've got lights, and things flashing, and the posters! Where I came from in Manchester, there was absolutely no. The only posters we got was on Friday when we got the weekly pamphlet from the church where we spent all our activities.[670]

*

The people aren't really any different, I think they're a little more on the ball in America because everything's *fast*! If you don't do it *right now* somebody else is going to jump in and do it before you, so you've got to do everything when you think about it. If you think about something, you do it right away, you don't wait because somebody else is going to come up with the idea.

I love America, you know, I love America almost as much as I love England, but I think [England] is the place to live. I want to end up here.

I was lucky when I went over [to America], it was a whole English thing; the English thing was really *in* and so I was treated nice. I wasn't a Monkee or anything, but I was on the stage and people treated me pretty good.[671]

*

UNITED STATES OF AMERICA
PERMANENT RESIDENT
Surname
JONES
Given Name
DAVID T
USCIS#
013-189-405
Category
Z2
Country of Birth
United Kingdom
Date of Birth
30 DEC 1945
Sex
M
Card Expires: 08/05/21
Resident Since: 06/12/63

Talk About War

People trying to conquer things only end up killing themselves.

That's a pity.

Me, I want to *help* them. I don't want to *kill* anybody… ever.".[672]

*

They won't get me, babe. Sure, they can legally draft me into the U.S. Army and send me to some jungle and order me to kill people. But I don't think it will happen.[673]

*

I was quite worried. [My draft status] was a big thing at the studio at the time. I paid lawyers and all kinds of stuff, but I came up with the answer.

I found out that being as short as I am, 5'4", you had to weigh over 104lbs. So I went down from my nine stone [126lbs] to 99lbs.

And I went down to the draft board and they did the same thing, stripped me naked and started prodding me, *cough cough*, all that stuff, (and I was new to all this stuff).

And I stood on the scales, and I thought, "This is it!" My little heart was going *boom-boom-boom!*

And this big guy said to me, "Boy, you're a 99lb weakling!"

And I said, "Right!" And fell over [with relief], you know what I mean?

And I stayed out the army, it was incredible.

And that's because of my height, being so short, I had to weigh over a certain amount, and that was the key.[674]

*

It's really a very upsetting thing to think about. I couldn't look at somebody and pull [a trigger], I couldn't even… I don't like to *touch* firearms, guns, because they scare me.

They say you gotta go out and fight for your country or whatever — if I see somebody standing in front of me with a gun, and it's either him or me, it's *me*, because I ain't gonna pull that trigger. I couldn't *live* after that, you know what I mean? But some people don't have any morals, I suppose.[675]

*

Are you asking if this whole thing [being drafted] is a publicity stunt? That would be a *terrible* thing! That'd be cheap and dirty! No, sir, it is *not* a publicity stunt. I wouldn't allow such a thing.[676]

*

I wouldn't chicken out of a fight. None of us would. Cowardice is not a funny subject. Neither is war.[677]

Talk About Zen

I can only relax gradually.

I think if I lie down to relax I still have the last thing that was on my mind going through my head. I never lie down and just *lie down* like most people, I'm always thinking, every minute.

I don't relax until I'm asleep.[678]

*

A hug a day. That's important for everybody. You must get hugged every day, everybody.[679]

Talk About The End

Summer 2011

I'm physically fit, and I'm pretty mentally active with other things in my life that take up my time. It's not easy. I did 46 concerts. I got home on Tuesday afternoon. On Wednesday, I drove to New York, which was a three and a half hour drive, and three and a half hours back, in order to be able to go on *The Joy Behar Show*, and then I drove back on Wednesday night. On Thursday morning, I got on a plane and flew to San Francisco. I was watching my daughter, yesterday, compete in a horse show at Pebble Beach. And this morning, I got on a plane, and I came here.

But I'm not feeling fatigued. I'm feeling, you know, "Hey, this is what I do," you know?[680]

*

December 2011

I feel better, my voice is better, I'm singing better, I'm feeling better about my life.[681]

*

I don't have to prove anything any more. I only have to say to myself: Am I having a good time? Yeah. Do I feel healthy? Yeah. Am I enjoying everything that I should be enjoying? Am

I comfortable in what I'm doing? Yeah. I am comfortable in what I'm doing.[682]

*

January, 2012

As I say: *never* give up your dream.
I haven't even *begun*![683]

*

January 28th, 2012

Had a WONDERFUL time [after performing aboard a cruise ship].[684]

*

February 2012

My doctor tells me I have the heart of a 25 year old.
Come visit me soon![685]

*

I don't want to be remembered as a Monkee or as the Artful Dodger or as an actor or as a singer or as a songwriter. I want to be remembered by each person differently. They all have something they can tell about, and things we've been intimate over, whether it be conversation or whether it be a kiss.

I want to retire unknown and anonymous and just fade away.

I want [my ashes] to be on a cruise ship or something… and I'll be overboard before anybody knows, and be eaten by a whale. I'll be back somewhere on some beach somewhere. When my kids go to the ocean I want them to know I'm there. So that would be kind of a romantic (legacy) in my way.[686]

*

The winters are so very hard in Pennsylvania that I make my way down south. I happen to stop almost at the end there in sunny Florida.[687]

*

Davy Jones suffered a heart attack on the morning of February 29th, 2012, at his property at Indiantown, Florida, after doing what he loved to do most in the whole world: ride his horses.

His earthly body was cremated, and after returning to Manchester, England, for a service at Lees Street Congregational Church in Openshaw — the same church in which he performed in plays as a child — his ashes were briefly placed on the grave of his mother and father.

His ashes were later scattered in the Atlantic Ocean.

A very strange thing happened just before my mother died. A few days before she passed away she cut a poem out of a magazine and she left it in her purse.

It's called "Love Still Abides."

He has passed on beyond the range of sight

Into the glory of the morning light

Out of the reach of sorrow and despair

Safe in the shelter of the Father's care

Weep not for him, say not he is dead

He has gone on a few short steps ahead

Faith looks beyond this time of grief and pain

Love still abides, and we shall meet again. [688]

Acknowledgements

The author would like to acknowledge the Davy Jones Equine Memorial Foundation (DJEMF), which was founded in 2012 by Davy's daughters, Talia, Sarah, Jessica, and Annabel, to protect and care for the herd of retired and rescued racehorses Davy left behind.

Today, the girls work to keep the remaining members of the herd healthy and safe with the generous support of friends, family, and fans. The Jones family is passionately committed to continuing Davy's equine advocacy work, and you can help by making purchases of Monkees related merchandise, and by becoming a horse sponsor or donor on the website haveyouherd.org

A portion of the proceeds from every sale of Have You Herd merchandise benefits the DJEMF herd and the organization's ongoing equine advocacy work.

If you found inspiration through the words of Davy Jones, please consider helping to take care of Davy's beloved herd of rescued racehorses.

Remember, they lost their dad, too.

*

A massive thanks to Johnny J Blair for contributing his in-depth *Foreword* full of memories and heart.

Johnny knew Davy for many years, and helped bring a lot of Davy's music into our lives, something for which the fans will be forever grateful. I know, because I am one of them.

I ask everyone to support Johnny and his own music through the following media links, where he also has a good amount of Monkees and Davy Jones solo material.

JJB website: http://johnnyjblairmusic.com

Bandcamp: https://johnnyjblairsingeratlarge.bandcamp.com

Patreon: https://www.patreon.com/johnnyjblair

Youtube: https://www.youtube.com/c/JohnnyJBlairSingeratLarge

*

I would also like to thank Davy, wherever you may be, for taking the time to share your words in an attempt help any and all fellow souls make their way through this dense human experience. It is my hope that this book will continue to allow your words to inspire others.

References

1 Living in TV Land, "Davy Jones Horsin' Around", 2006

2 "Davy Talks About Acting", Tiger *Beat*, November 1967

3 "Davy Talks About Acting", Tiger *Beat*, November 1967

4 Spin Cycle Post, *Daydream Believers DVD*, 14 November 2001

5 Bernstein, A, "Interview with Monkees member Davy Jones on MUSIC: 60s POP ROCK" by A Bernstein, Assignment x, 2 Dec 2011

6 "Davy Talks About Acting", Tiger *Beat*, November 1967

7 "Davy Talks About Acting", Tiger *Beat*, November 1967

8 Spin Cycle Post, *Daydream Believers DVD*, 14 November 2001

9 Spatz, D, "Curtain Call with Davy Jones", 1994

10 Burns, M, Profiles Featuring Davy Jones. 7 Apr 2010

11 Spin Cycle Post, *Daydream Believers DVD*, 14 November 2001

12 "Davy Jones Interview: Monkees/Memoir", Reelin' In The Years, 1988

13 "Davy Jones Interview: Monkees/Memoir", Reelin' In The Years, 1988

14 Spatz, D, "Curtain Call with Davy Jones", 1994

15 British Film Institute, www.youtube.com/watch?v=SsZcs_4Nznc, 1968

16 Spin Cycle Post, *Daydream Believers DVD*, 14 November 2001

17 "Davy Jones Answers the Questions You've Been Asking", Monkee Spectacular, May 1968

18 "Davy Talks About Acting", Tiger *Beat*, November 1967

19 Johnny J. Blair, Billtown Bus Stop Radio Hour, 7 Dec 2009

20 Spin Cycle Post, *Daydream Believers DVD*, 14 November 2001

21 Harris, D, "Retro Rewind, Conversation with Davy Jones", 2008

22 British Film Institute, www.youtube.com/watch?v=SsZcs_4Nznc, 1968

23 British Film Institute, www.youtube.com/watch?v=SsZcs_4Nznc, 1968

24 The Original 70's Soundtrack, Alan Barnes and Sue Steward, 96.5 WCTG.FM, November 2010

25 The Monkees, Davy Jones Last San Diego Interview with Kevin Fulton, Blog This & Presido Sentinel

26 "Davy Jones Interview: Monkees/Memoir", Reelin' In The Years, 1988

27 Harper, S, "The Monkees: Davy Jones In Conversation: Our salute to a pop great." www.clashmusic.com/features/the-monkees-davy-jones-in-conversation

28 *Monkee Spectacular*, April 1967

29 Johnny J. Blair, Billtown Bus Stop Radio Hour, 7 Dec 2009

30 Spatz, D, "Curtain Call with Davy Jones", 1994

31 "Davy Jones: "Being a Monkee Has Been My Greatest Success so Far"", Monkee Spectacular Reprint, 1987

32 The Monkees, Davy Jones Last San Diego Interview with Kevin Fulton, Blog This & Presido Sentinel

33 "Monkees Davy Jones," Good Morning San Diego, 31 December 2011

34 Spatz, D, "Curtain Call with Davy Jones", 1994

35 Living in TV Land, "Davy Jones Horsin' Around", 2006

36 2012, Gloabal Recording Artists and Fatbelly Productions

37 Moses, A, *Tiger Beat*, July 1968

38 Daydream Believers DVD Commentary

39 Harris, D, "Retro Rewind, Conversation with Davy Jones", 2008

40 Fantaskey Kazuba, B,"Monkee in the Middle of Nowhere", The Best of Central PA 2000 magazine, December 2000

41 "Wild 2000 phone interview with Davy Jones of The Monkees", Beyond Vaudeville, 2000

42 Harper, S, "The Monkees: Davy Jones In Conversation: Our salute to a pop great."www.clashmusic.com/features/the-monkees-davy-jones-in-conversation

43 James, G, "Interview With Davy Jones Of The Monkees:, www.classicbands.com/DavyJonesInterview.html

44 "Davy Jones Interview: Monkees/Memoir", Reelin' In The Years, 1988

45 "Davy Jones Interview: Monkees/Memoir", Reelin' In The Years, 1988

46 Dakota Radio, Live Radio Show Deadwood, 21 October 2011

47 "Wild 2000 phone interview with Davy Jones of The Monkees", Beyond Vaudeville, 2000

48 Harris, D, "Retro Rewind, Conversation with Davy Jones", 2008

49 Harris, D, "Retro Rewind, Conversation with Davy Jones", 2008

50 Dakota Radio, Live Radio Show Deadwood, 21 October 2011

51 2001: Live in Las Vegas!, 2001

52 Jones, D, Spin Cycle Post, *Daydream Believers DVD*, 14 November 2001

53 The Original 70's Soundtrack, Alan Barnes and Sue Steward, 96.5 WCTG.FM, November 2010

54 "Davy Jones Reveals All: His Guest Shot on The Brady Bunch and Marcia Brady", Pop Goes The Culture TV

55 Moses, A, *Tiger Beat*, July 1968

56 Real Crime: The REELZ Files Podcast, "Autopsy: The Last Hours of Davy Jones", 11 Jul 2022

57 *Tiger Beat*, January 1967

58 "Davy Talks About Acting", Tiger *Beat*, November 1967

59 "Davy Talks About Acting", Tiger *Beat*, November 1967

60 *Tiger Beat*, January 1967

61 *Tiger Beat*, January 1967

62 Baker, A, "Monkee Mania", 1989

63 Davy Jones: Horsin' Around; Living in TV Land, 2006

64 Milham, S, "How a racing-mad Monkee is repaying a debt of gratitude to a retired Newmarket trainer," [updated 17 Feb, 2012]

65 Baker, A, "Monkee Mania", 1989

66 Milham, S, "How a racing-mad Monkee is repaying a debt of gratitude to a retired Newmarket trainer," [updated 17 Feb, 2012] .

67 *Tiger Beat*, January 1967

68 *Tiger Beat*, January 1967

69 "Davy Jones Interview: Monkees/Memoir", Reelin' In The Years, 1988

70 Real Crime: The REELZ Files Podcast, "Autopsy: The Last Hours of Davy Jones", 11 Jul 2022

71 "Davy Jones Faces Viet Nam and Says: I Don't Want to Kill Anybody", *Teen Life*, Aug 1967

72 "Davy Talks About Acting", Tiger *Beat*, November 1967

73 *Tiger Beat*, January 1967

74 Milham, S, "How a racing-mad Monkee is repaying a debt of gratitude to a retired Newmarket trainer," [updated 17 Feb, 2012]

75 Davy Jones: Horsin' Around; Living in TV Land, 2006

76 Baker, A, "Monkee Mania", 1989

77 Harris, W, "Rescued from the Archives: Remembering Mr. Jones: Farewell to a Monkee," That Thing They Did, 2012

78 Jones, D, Spin Cycle Post, *Daydream Believers DVD*, 14 November 2001

79 Harris, W, "Rescued from the Archives: Remembering Mr. Jones: Farewell to a Monkee," That Thing They Did, 2012

80 *Tiger Beat*, January 1967

81 Harris, W, "Rescued from the Archives: Remembering Mr. Jones: Farewell to a Monkee," That Thing They Did, 2012

82 *Tiger Beat Presents Davy Jones*, December 1967

83 Harris, W, "Rescued from the Archives: Remembering Mr. Jones: Farewell to a Monkee," That Thing They Did, 2012

84 *Tiger Beat Presents Davy Jones*, December 1967

85 *Tiger Beat Presents Davy Jones*, December 1967

86 *Tiger Beat*, January 1967

87 Davy Jones Interview, Youtube

88 Harris, W, "Rescued from the Archives: Remembering Mr. Jones: Farewell to a Monkee," That Thing They Did, 2012

89 Robbins, C, "Hey Hey It's The Monkees' Davy Jones", *BWW Interviews*, 25 Aug 25, 2011

90 Wentworth, J, KCOW radio, 2011

91 Jones, D, Spin Cycle Post, *Daydream Believers DVD*, 14 November 2001

92 *Tiger Beat*, January 1967

93 Baker, A, "Monkee Mania", 1989

94 Milham, S, "How a racing-mad Monkee is repaying a debt of gratitude to a retired Newmarket trainer," [updated 17 Feb, 2012]

95 Bernstein, A, "Interview with Monkees member Davy Jones on MUSIC: 60s POP ROCK" by A Bernstein, Assignment x, 2 Dec 2011

96 Robbins, C, "Hey Hey It's The Monkees' Davy Jones", *BWW Interviews*, 25 Aug 25, 2011

97 Spatz, D, "Curtain Call with Davy Jones", 1994

98 Robbins, C, "Hey Hey It's The Monkees' Davy Jones", *BWW Interviews*, 25 Aug 25, 2011

99 Getlen, L, "Fame & Fortune: Davy Jones", Bankrate

100 Wentworth, J, KCOW radio, 2011

101 "Davy Jones: "Being a Monkee Has Been My Greatest Success so Far"", Monkee Spectacular Reprint, 1987

102 "Davy Remembers His Mother", *Tiger Beat*, May 1968

103 Jones, D, 16 Magazine, March 1967

104 *Tiger Beat*, January 1967

105 *Tiger Beat*, January 1967

106 *Tiger Beat*, January 1967

107 British Film Institute, www.youtube.com/watch?
v=SsZcs_4Nznc, 1968

108 Jones, D, "Davy Jones: Where are they now, Australia",
2007

109 Harper, S, "The Monkees: Davy Jones In Conversation:
Our salute to a pop great."www.clashmusic.com/features/
the-monkees-davy-jones-in-conversation

110 Baker, A, "Monkee Mania", 1989

111 Spin Cycle Post, *Daydream Believers DVD*, 14 November
2001

112 Spatz, D, "Curtain Call with Davy Jones", 1994

113 "Hey, Hey, We're The Monkees", Harold Bronson, 1996

114 Daydream Believers DVD Commentary

115 Johnny J. Blair, Billtown Bus Stop Radio Hour, 7 Dec
2009

116 Daydream Believers DVD Commentary

117 www.chroniclelive.co.uk/whats-on/music/interview-
davy-jones-monkees-1398185

118 "Hey, Hey, We're The Monkees", Harold Bronson, 1996

119 Daydream Believers DVD Commentary

120 *16 Magazine*, March 1968

121 James, G, "Interview With Davy Jones Of The Monkees:, www.classicbands.com/DavyJonesInterview.html

122 Celebrity Interview Davy Jones, www.celebrityparentsmag.com/parenting/celebrity-interview-the-monkees-davy-jones

123 "Davy Jones Answers the Questions You've Been Asking" Monkee Spectacular, May 1968

124 Das, L, "What A Cheeky Monkee", May 2011

125 Harris, D, "Retro Rewind, Conversation with Davy Jones", 2008

126 Spatz, D, "Curtain Call with Davy Jones", 1994

127 https://www.youtube.com/watch?v=UUVu7oec6rg

128 Harris, D, "Retro Rewind, Conversation with Davy Jones", 2008

129 Harris, D, "Retro Rewind, Conversation with Davy Jones", 2008

130 Bernstein, A, "Interview with Monkees member Davy Jones on MUSIC: 60s POP ROCK" by A Bernstein, Assignment x, 2 Dec 2011

131 Fantaskey Kazuba, B,"Monkee in the Middle of Nowhere", The Best of Central PA 2000 magazine, December 2000

132 The Original 70's Soundtrack, Alan Barnes and Sue Steward, 96.5 WCTG.FM, November 2010

133 Davy Jones: Horsin' Around; Living in TV Land, 2006

134 "The Monkees - Davy Jones/Biography", YouTube

135 Walters, B, Styleweekly, May 12, 2004

136 Fantaskey Kazuba, B,"Monkee in the Middle of Nowhere", The Best of Central PA 2000 magazine, December 2000

137 Bailey, Rob, "David vs. Davy", Back Talk, www.silive.com/entertainment/music/2008/09/, Sep 2008

138 The Monkees, Davy Jones Last San Diego Interview with Kevin Fulton, Blog This & Presido Sentinel

139 Getlen, L, "Fame & Fortune: Davy Jones", Bankrate

140 Newsom, J, "Davy Jones: The Way You Hoped He'd Be", Veem Magazine, October 15, 2011

141 Daydream Believers DVD Commentary

142 Overbea, L, "Monkees: Hard workers with varied opinions"

143 Moses, A, *Tiger Beat*, July 1968

144 Moses, A, *Tiger Beat*, July 1968

145 Johnny J. Blair, Billtown Bus Stop Radio Hour, 7 Dec 2009

146 "Wild 2000 phone interview with Davy Jones of The Monkees", Beyond Vaudeville, 2000

147 Harris, D, "Retro Rewind, Conversation with Davy Jones", 2008

148 Harris, D, "Retro Rewind, Conversation with Davy Jones", 2008

149 Spin Cycle Post, *Daydream Believers DVD*, 14 November 2001

150 Davy and Sarah Jones on Pebble Mill, March 1997

151 https://www.youtube.com/watch?v=UUVu7oec6rg

152 https://www.youtube.com/watch?v=UUVu7oec6rg

153 https://www.youtube.com/watch?v=UUVu7oec6rg

154 https://www.youtube.com/watch?v=UUVu7oec6rg

155 Harper, S, "The Monkees: Davy Jones In Conversation: Our salute to a pop great." www.clashmusic.com/features/the-monkees-davy-jones-in-conversation

156 "Sally Jessy Raphael", 1993

157 Spin Cycle Post, *Daydream Believers DVD*, 14 November 2001

158 Fantaskey Kazuba, B,"Monkee in the Middle of Nowhere", The Best of Central PA 2000 magazine, December 2000

159 Spin Cycle Post, *Daydream Believers DVD*, 14 November 2001

160 Harris, W, "Rescued from the Archives: Remembering Mr. Jones: Farewell to a Monkee," That Thing They Did, 2012

161 Johnny J. Blair, Billtown Bus Stop Radio Hour, 7 Dec 2009

162 Dakota Radio, Live Radio Show Deadwood, 21 October 2011

163 "Davy Remembers His Mother", *Tiger Beat*, May 1968

164 "Autopsy, The Last Hours of Davy Jones", The Reels files

165 "Davy Remembers His Mother", *Tiger Beat*, May 1968

166 "Davy Remembers His Mother", *Tiger Beat*, May 1968

167 "Davy Remembers His Mother", *Tiger Beat*, May 1968

168 "Davy Remembers His Mother", *Tiger Beat*, May 1968

169 Baker, A, "Monkee Mania", 1989

170 "Davy Jones Faces Viet Nam and Says: I Don't Want to Kill Anybody", *Teen Life*, Aug 1967

171 Baker, A, "Monkee Mania", 1989

172 Jones, D, British Film Institute, www.youtube.com/watch?v=SsZcs_4Nznc, 1968

173 "Davy Remembers His Mother", *Tiger Beat*, May 1968

174 *Tiger Beat*, April 1967

175 *16 Magazine*, May 1968

176 Daydream Believers DVD Commentary

177 www.chroniclelive.co.uk/whats-on/music/interview-davy-jones-monkees-1398185

178 Milham, S, "How a racing-mad Monkee is repaying a debt of gratitude to a retired Newmarket trainer," [updated 17 Feb, 2012]

179 Creative Illusions Productions, 2008, https://www.youtube.com/watch?v=CRpN_WLN6PQ,

180 *Monkee Spectacular*, April 1967

181 *Monkee Spectacular*, April 1967

182 Moses, A, *Tiger Beat*, July 1968

183 Moses, A, *Tiger Beat*, July 1968

184 Moses, A, *Tiger Beat*, July 1968

185 Celebrity Interview Davy Jones, www.celebrityparentsmag.com/parenting/celebrity-interview-the-monkees-davy-jones

186 Davy Jones and Micky Dolenz on The Ed Bernstein Show, 3 April 2001

187 Davy Jones: Horsin' Around; Living in TV Land, 2006

188 Davy Jones: Horsin' Around; Living in TV Land, 2006

189 Davy Jones: Horsin' Around; Living in TV Land, 2006

190 Davy Jones: Horsin' Around; Living in TV Land, 2006

191 Hunniford, G, Celebs Up Close with Gloria Hunniford, 1984

192 www.philmusic.charmingflowers.com.vn/surprising-news-a-cut-interview-with-davy-jones-from-1997-just-surfaced-in-which-he-revealed-that

193 *Tiger Beat*, August 1968

194 James, G, "Interview With Davy Jones Of The Monkees:, www.classicbands.com/DavyJonesInterview.html

195 Daydream Believers DVD Commentary

196 "Davy Jones: Where are they now, Australia", 2007

197 Davy Jones: Horsin' Around; Living in TV Land, 2006

198 "Davy Jones Interview: Monkees/Memoir", Reelin' In The Years, 1988

199 The Original 70's Soundtrack, Alan Barnes and Sue Steward, 96.5 WCTG.FM, November 2010

200 PCA Interview, 2006

201 Harris, D, "Retro Rewind, Conversation with Davy Jones", 2008

202 "Davy Jones Answers the Questions You've Been Asking" Monkee Spectacular, May 1968

203 Spin Cycle Post, *Daydream Believers DVD*, 14 November 2001

204 "Davy Remembers His Mother", *Tiger Beat*, May 1968

205 "Davy Talking on the Transatlantic Phone", *Monkees Monthly*, Oct 1968

206 Live at BB King Club, New York, Feb 2012

207 Baked Zucchini Recipe with Florence Henderson, Country Kitchen, April 1991

208 Benner, R, "Monkee Recipes", Monkee Spectactular, March 1968

209 Stevenson, S, "Monkee Food", Monkee Spectactular, August 1967

210 https://celebrityparentsmag.com/celebrity-recipes/this-old-soup-recipe-from-the-monkees-davy-jones-will-make-you-a-believer/

211 Benner, R, "Monkee Recipes", Monkee Spectactular, February 1968

212 Dakota Radio, Live Radio Show Deadwood, 21 October 2011

213 Head DVD Commentary

214 Harris, D, "Retro Rewind, Conversation with Davy Jones", 2008

215 Jenel Smith, S, "Hey, Hey, Monkees Fans", AARP, 1 Dec 2011

216 Bernstein, A, "Interview with Monkees member Davy Jones on MUSIC: 60s POP ROCK" by A Bernstein, Assignment x, 2 Dec 2011

217 Celebrity Interview Davy Jones, www.celebrityparentsmag.com/parenting/celebrity-interview-the-monkees-davy-jones

218 Robbins, C, "Hey Hey It's The Monkees' Davy Jones", *BWW Interviews*, 25 Aug 25, 2011

219 Jenel Smith, S, "Hey, Hey, Monkees Fans", AARP, 1 Dec 2011

220 Live at BB King Club, New York, Feb 2012

221 "Monkees Davy Jones," Good Morning San Diego, 31 December 2011

222 Davy Jones: Horsin' Around; Living in TV Land, 2006

223 Bernstein, A, "Interview with Monkees member Davy Jones on MUSIC: 60s POP ROCK" by A Bernstein, Assignment x, 2 Dec 2011

224 Celebrity Interview Davy Jones, www.celebrityparentsmag.com/parenting/celebrity-interview-the-monkees-davy-jones

225 "Davy Jones Interview: Monkees/Memoir", Reelin' In The Years, 1988

226 Newsom, J, "Davy Jones: The Way You Hoped He'd Be", Veem Magazine, 15 October 2011

227 "Monkees Davy Jones," Good Morning San Diego, 31 December 2011

228 Jones, D, "Davy Jones Interview: Monkees/Memoir", Reelin' In The Years, 1988

229 Davy Jones: Horsin' Around; Living in TV Land, 2006

230 *Tiger Beat*, July 1968

231 *16 Magazine*, July 1968

232 *Tiger Beat*, January 1967

233 "Davy Talks Frankly About All the Girls in His Life" Tiger Beat, March 1968

234 Harris, W, "Rescued from the Archives: Remembering Mr. Jones: Farewell to a Monkee," That Thing They Did, 2012

235 Baker, A, "Monkee Mania", 1989

236 "Davy Talks Frankly About All the Girls in His Life" Tiger Beat, March 1968

237 "Davy Talks Frankly About All the Girls in His Life" Tiger Beat, March 1968

238 "Davy Talks Frankly About All the Girls in His Life" Tiger Beat, March 1968

239 "Davy Talks Frankly About All the Girls in His Life" Tiger Beat, March 1968

240 Fantaskey Kazuba, B,"Monkee in the Middle of Nowhere", The Best of Central PA 2000 magazine, December 2000

241 Jones, D, Real Deal Bob Steal, March 2001

242 Getlen, L, "Fame & Fortune: Davy Jones", Bankrate

243 Getlen, L, "Fame & Fortune: Davy Jones", Bankrate

244 *People Magazine*, 27 July 27 1992

245 The Monkees - Davy Jones/Biography, YouTube

246 The Howard Stern Show, April 1992

247 *People Magazine*, 27 July 27 1992

248 Hunniford, G, Celebs Up Close with Gloria Hunniford, 1984

249 The Original 70's Soundtrack, Alan Barnes and Sue Steward, 96.5 WCTG.FM, November 2010

250 www.chroniclelive.co.uk/whats-on/music/interview-davy-jones-monkees-1398185

251 The Original 70's Soundtrack, Alan Barnes and Sue Steward, 96.5 WCTG.FM, November 2010

252 Fantaskey Kazuba, B,"Monkee in the Middle of Nowhere", The Best of Central PA 2000 magazine, December 2000

253 Das L, Dailymail, 2011

254 Milham, S, "How a racing-mad Monkee is repaying a debt of gratitude to a retired Newmarket trainer," [updated 17 Feb, 2012]

255 Milham, S, "How a racing-mad Monkee is repaying a debt of gratitude to a retired Newmarket trainer," [updated 17 Feb, 2012]

256 "Davy Talks About Acting", *Tiger Beat*, Nov 1967

257 Burns, M, Profiles Featuring Davy Jones. 7 Apr 2010

258 "The Littlest Monkee Is Still Going Strong", Chicago Tribune, 28 January 2011

259 Robbins, C, "Hey Hey It's The Monkees' Davy Jones", *BWW Interviews*, 25 Aug 25, 2011

260 "Davy Remembers His Mother", *Tiger Beat*, May 1968

261 "Davy Remembers His Mother", *Tiger Beat*, May 1968

262 "Davy Remembers His Mother", *Tiger Beat*, May 1968

263 Das, L, "What A Cheeky Monkee", May 2011

264 "Davy Remembers His Mother", *Tiger Beat*, May 1968

265 Baker, A, "Monkee Mania", 1989

266 "Davy Jones Answers the Questions You've Been Asking" Monkee Spectacular, May 1968**

267 Harper, S, "The Monkees: Davy Jones In Conversation: Our salute to a pop great." www.clashmusic.com/features/the-monkees-davy-jones-in-conversation

268 "Davy Jones Answers the Questions You've Been Asking" Monkee Spectacular, May 1968**

269 Harris, D, "Retro Rewind, Conversation with Davy Jones", 2008

270 Celebrity Interview Davy Jones, www.celebrityparentsmag.com/parenting/celebrity-interview-the-monkees-davy-jones

271 Moses, A, *Tiger Beat*, July 1968

272 Daydream Believers DVD Commentary

273 The Monkees, Davy Jones Last San Diego Interview with Kevin Fulton, Blog This & Presido Sentinel

274 "Davy Jones of The Monkees", Pop Goes the Culture TV

275 Moses, A, *Tiger Beat*, July 1968

276 "Davy Jones Answers the Questions You've Been Asking" Monkee Spectacular, May 1968

277 https://www.youtube.com/watch?v=UUVu7oec6rg

278 Davy Jones: Horsin' Around; Living in TV Land, 2006

279 Spin Cycle Post, *Daydream Believers DVD*, 14 November 2001

280 "Monkees Davy Jones," Good Morning San Diego, 31 December 2011

281 Bernstein, A, "Interview with Monkees member Davy Jones on MUSIC: 60s POP ROCK" by A Bernstein, Assignment x, 2 Dec 2011

282 Milham, S, "How a racing-mad Monkee is repaying a debt of gratitude to a retired Newmarket trainer," [updated 17 Feb, 2012]

283 Milham, S, "How a racing-mad Monkee is repaying a debt of gratitude to a retired Newmarket trainer," [updated 17 Feb, 2012]

284 www.chroniclelive.co.uk/whats-on/music/interview-davy-jones-monkees-1398185

285 Spin Cycle Post, *Daydream Believers DVD*, 14 November 2001

286 "Davy Jones Interview: Monkees/Memoir", Reelin' In The Years, 1988

287 Davy Jones: Horsin' Around; Living in TV Land, 2006

288 Davy Jones: Horsin' Around; Living in TV Land, 2006

289 Davy Jones: Horsin' Around; Living in TV Land, 2006

290 Davy Jones: Horsin' Around; Living in TV Land, 2006

291 Davy Jones: Horsin' Around; Living in TV Land, 2006

292 Walters, B, Styleweekly, May 12, 2004

293 Walters, B, Styleweekly, May 12, 2004

294 Walters, B, Styleweekly, May 12, 2004

295 Milham, S, "How a racing-mad Monkee is repaying a debt of gratitude to a retired Newmarket trainer," [updated 17 Feb, 2012]

296 Walters, B, Styleweekly, May 12, 2004

297 Das L, Dailymail, 2011

298 Robbins, C, "Hey Hey It's The Monkees' Davy Jones", *BWW Interviews*, 25 Aug 25, 2011

299 Dakota Radio, Live Radio Show Deadwood, 21 October 2011

300 Live at BB King Club, New York, Feb 2012

301 Live at BB King Club, New York, Feb 2012

302 Live at BB King Club, New York, Feb 2012

303 Lina Das, Mailonline

304 Daily Mail, May 2011

305 Star Plaza Live, 2011

306 Real Deal Bob Steal, March 2001

307 "Hey, Hey, We're The Monkees", Harold Bronson, 1996

308 "This Is Your Life: Harry Secombe," 1990

309 Live at BB King Club, New York, Feb 2012

310 Star Plaza Live, 2011

311 Live at BB King Club, New York, Feb 2012

312 Johnny J. Blair, Billtown Bus Stop Radio Hour, 7 Dec 2009

313 Wentworth, J, KCOW radio, 2011

314 Daydream Believers DVD Commentary

315 Johnny J. Blair, Billtown Bus Stop Radio Hour, 7 Dec 2009

316 Spatz, D, "Curtain Call with Davy Jones", 1994

317 Spatz, D, "Curtain Call with Davy Jones", 1994

318 "Hey, Hey, We're The Monkees", Harold Bronson, 1996

319 Bailey, Rob, "David vs. Davy", Back Talk, www.silive.com/entertainment/music/2008/09/, Sep 2008

320 Live at BB King Club, New York, Feb 2012

321 Das L, Dailymail, 2011

322 Harris, D, "Retro Rewind, Conversation with Davy Jones", 2008

323 James, G, "Interview With Davy Jones Of The Monkees:, www.classicbands.com/DavyJonesInterview.html

324 "Wild 2000 phone interview with Davy Jones of The Monkees", Beyond Vaudeville, 2000

325 www.philmusic.charmingflowers.com.vn/surprising-news-a-cut-interview-with-davy-jones-from-1997-just-surfaced-in-which-he-revealed-that

326 https://www.youtube.com/watch?v=UUVu7oec6rg

327 Jenel Smith, S, "Hey, Hey, Monkees Fans", AARP, 1 Dec 2011

328 "Davy Jones of The Monkees", Pop Goes the Culture TV

329 "Davy Jones of The Monkees", Pop Goes the Culture TV

330 "Davy Jones Interview", Forgotten Media, 1988

331 Davy Jones: Horsin' Around; Living in TV Land, 2006

332 Spin Cycle Post, *Daydream Believers DVD*, 14 November 2001

333 That Thing They Did by Will Harris, "Rescued from the Archives: Remembering Mr. Jones: Farewell to a Monkee", Mar, 2012

334 Dakota Radio, Live Radio Show Deadwood, 21 October 2011

335 Walters, B, Styleweekly, May 12, 2004

336 Real Deal Bob Steal, March 2001

337 Moses, A, *Tiger Beat*, July 1968

338 Newsom, J, "Davy Jones: The Way You Hoped He'd Be", Veem Magazine, October 15, 2011

339 Live at BB King Club, New York, Feb 2012

340 Real Deal Bob Steal, March 2001

341 Harris, D, "Retro Rewind, Conversation with Davy Jones", 2008

342 PCA Interview, 2006

343 "Davy Talks Frankly About All the Girls in His Life" Tiger Beat, March 1968

344 "Davy Talks Frankly About All the Girls in His Life" Tiger Beat, March 1968

345 *Monkee Spectacular*, April 1967

346 *Monkee Spectacular*, April 1967

347 Daydream Believers DVD Commentary

348 Das, L, "What A Cheeky Monkee", May 2011

349 Das, L, "What A Cheeky Monkee", May 2011

350 Das, L, "What A Cheeky Monkee", May 2011

351 Das, L, "What A Cheeky Monkee", May 2011

352 Celebrity Interview Davy Jones, www.celebrityparentsmag.com/parenting/celebrity-interview-the-monkees-davy-jones

353 Das, L, "What A Cheeky Monkee", May 2011

354 Celebrity Interview Davy Jones, www.celebrityparentsmag.com/parenting/celebrity-interview-the-monkees-davy-jones

355 The Monkees, Davy Jones Last San Diego Interview with Kevin Fulton, Blog This & Presido Sentinel

356 Das, L, "What A Cheeky Monkee", May 2011

357 "Hey, Hey, We're The Monkees", Harold Bronson, 1996

358 *Tiger Beat Presents Davy Jones*, December 1967

359 Harper, S, "The Monkees: Davy Jones In Conversation: Our salute to a pop great." www.clashmusic.com/features/the-monkees-davy-jones-in-conversation

360 The Monkees - Davy Jones/Biography, YouTube

361 Daydream Believers DVD Commentary

362 *Tiger Beat Presents Davy Jones*, December 1967

363 Daydream Believers DVD Commentary

364 Moses, A, *Tiger Beat*, July 1968

365 Daydream Believers DVD Commentary

366 Lina Das, Mailonline

367 The Monkees - Davy Jones/Biography, YouTube

368 Daydream Believers DVD Commentary

369 Davy and Sarah Jones on Pebble Mill, March 1997

370 Daydream Believers DVD Commentary

371 "Hey, Hey, We're The Monkees", Harold Bronson, 1996

372 Daydream Believers DVD Commentary

373 Daydream Believers DVD Commentary

374 Daydream Believers DVD Commentary

375 Daydream Believers DVD Commentary

376 www.chroniclelive.co.uk/whats-on/music/interview-davy-jones-monkees-1398185

377 Lina Das, Mailonline

378 Live at BB King Club, New York, 18 Feb 2012

379 "Davy Talking on the Transatlantic Phone", *Monkees Monthly*, Oct 1968

380 Getlen, L, "Fame & Fortune: Davy Jones", Bankrate

381 The Monkees - Davy Jones/Biography, YouTube

382 The Monkees - Davy Jones/Biography, YouTube

383 Daydream Believers DVD, November 2001

384 Daydream Believers DVD, November 2001

385 The Howard Stern Show, April 1992

386 Daydream Believers DVD Commentary

387 The Howard Stern Show, April 1992

388 The Howard Stern Show, April 1992

389 The Rosie O'Donnell Show, 1996

390 Simpson, O, "Davy Jones Attacks Monkees bandmates", 08 Oct 2009

391 "The Littlest Monkee Is Still Going Strong", Chicago Tribune, 28 January 2011

[392] Daydream Believers DVD Commentary

[393] The Ed Bernstein Show, 3 April 2001

[394] Daydream Believers DVD Commentary

[395] Daydream Believers DVD Commentary

[396] Live at BB King Club, New York, Feb 2012

[397] Daydream Believers DVD Commentary

[398] Cortez, C, "In Memorium - One of the last interviews with The Monkees' Davy Jones", original interview summer 2011

[399] "The Monkees - Davy Jones/Biography", YouTube

[400] Daydream Believers DVD Commentary

[401] "Hey, Hey, We're The Monkees", Harold Bronson, 1996

[402] Spin Cycle Post, *Daydream Believers DVD*, 14 November 2001

[403] Daydream Believers DVD Commentary

[404] Simpson, O, "Davy Jones Attacks Monkees bandmates", 08 Oct 2009

[405] Daydream Believers DVD Commentary

[406] Daydream Believers DVD Commentary

[407] *Tiger Beat*, January 1967

[408] "Davy Remembers His Mother", *Tiger Beat*, May 1968

409 British Film Institute, www.youtube.com/watch?v=SsZcs_4Nznc, 1968

410 British Film Institute, www.youtube.com/watch?v=SsZcs_4Nznc, 1968

411 British Film Institute, www.youtube.com/watch?v=SsZcs_4Nznc, 1968

412 Baker, A, "Monkee Mania", 1989

413 Baker, A, "Monkee Mania", 1989

414 Harper, S, "The Monkees: Davy Jones In Conversation: Our salute to a pop great. www.clashmusic.com/features/the-monkees-davy-jones-in-conversation

415 Harper, S, "The Monkees: Davy Jones In Conversation: Our salute to a pop great." www.clashmusic.com/features/the-monkees-davy-jones-in-conversation

416 James, G, "Interview With Davy Jones Of The Monkees:, www.classicbands.com/DavyJonesInterview.html

417 British Film Institute, www.youtube.com/watch?v=SsZcs_4Nznc, 1968

418 Burns, M, Profiles Featuring Davy Jones. 7 Apr 2010

419 Getlen, L, "Fame & Fortune: Davy Jones", Bankrate

420 The Jones Boy is Now the Jones Man by Joan Crosby, 1972

421 James, G, "Interview With Davy Jones Of The Monkees:, www.classicbands.com/DavyJonesInterview.html

422 James, G, "Interview With Davy Jones Of The Monkees:, www.classicbands.com/DavyJonesInterview.html

423 https://www.youtube.com/watch?v=UUVu7oec6rg

424 "Davy Jones Interview: Monkees/Memoir", Reelin' In The Years, 1988

425 The Original 70's Soundtrack, Alan Barnes and Sue Steward, 96.5 WCTG.FM, November 2010

426 British Film Institute, www.youtube.com/watch?v=SsZcs_4Nznc, 1968

427 Celebrity Interview Davy Jones, www.celebrityparentsmag.com/parenting/celebrity-interview-the-monkees-davy-jones

428 Simpson, O, "Davy Jones Attacks Monkees bandmates", 08 Oct 2009

429 https://www.youtube.com/watch?v=UUVu7oec6rg

430 Baker, A, "Monkee Mania", 1989

431 Harper, S, "The Monkees: Davy Jones In Conversation: Our salute to a pop great."www.clashmusic.com/features/the-monkees-davy-jones-in-conversation

432 Spin Cycle Post, *Daydream Believers DVD*, 14 November 2001

433 Hunniford, G, Celebs Up Close with Gloria Hunniford, 1984

434 British Film Institute, www.youtube.com/watch?v=SsZcs_4Nznc, 1968

435 Baker, A, "Monkee Mania", 1989

436 "Hey, Hey, We're The Monkees", Harold Bronson, 1996

437 Daydream Believers DVD Commentary

438 Spatz, D, "Curtain Call with Davy Jones", 1994

439 Baker, A, "Monkee Mania", 1989

440 "Monkees Davy Jones," Good Morning San Diego, 31 December 2011

441 Spin Cycle Post, *Daydream Believers DVD*, 14 November 2001

442 *16 Magazine*, February 1967

443 Spin Cycle Post, *Daydream Believers DVD*, 14 November 2001

444 Jones, D, Daydream Believers DVD Commentary

445 Baker, A, "Monkee Mania", 1989

446 Getlen, L, "Fame & Fortune: Davy Jones", Bankrate

447 Daydream Believers DVD, November 2001

448 Getlen, L, "Fame & Fortune: Davy Jones", Bankrate

449 Jones, D, Spin Cycle Post, *Daydream Believers DVD*, 14 November 2001

450 "Hey, Hey, We're The Monkees", Harold Bronson, 1996

451 Daydream Believers DVD Commentary

452 "Hey, Hey, We're The Monkees", Harold Bronson, 1996

453 "Hey, Hey, We're The Monkees", Harold Bronson, 1996

454 Daydream Believers DVD Commentary

455 Daydream Believers DVD Commentary

456 "Davy Jones Interview: Monkees/Memoir", Reelin' In The Years, 1988

457 Daydream Believers DVD Commentary

458 Roch Parisien's Rocon Communications, October 1990

459 Hunniford, G, Celebs Up Close with Gloria Hunniford, 1984

460 "Hey, Hey, We're The Monkees", Harold Bronson, 1996

461 Baker, A, "Monkee Mania", 1989

462 James, G, "Interview With Davy Jones Of The Monkees:, www.classicbands.com/DavyJonesInterview.html

463 Daydream Believers DVD Commentary

464 Ask Jimmy Carter", https://www.youtube.com/watch?v=UUVu7oec6rg

465 British Film Institute, www.youtube.com/watch?v=SsZcs_4Nznc, 1968

466 Dakota Radio, Live Radio Show Deadwood, 21 October 2011

467 Jones, D, Daydream Believers DVD Commentary

468 Baker, A, "Monkee Mania", 1989

469 "Hey, Hey, We're The Monkees", Harold Bronson, 1996

470 *Tiger Beat*, January 1967

471 Daydream Believers DVD Commentary

472 Daydream Believers DVD Commentary

473 Daydream Believers DVD Commentary

474 Harper, S, "The Monkees: Davy Jones In Conversation: Our salute to a pop great." www.clashmusic.com/features/the-monkees-davy-jones-in-conversation

475 Daydream Believers DVD Commentary

476 Daydream Believers DVD Commentary

477 Daydream Believers DVD Commentary

478 Harper, S, "The Monkees: Davy Jones In Conversation: Our salute to a pop great." www.clashmusic.com/features/the-monkees-davy-jones-in-conversation

479 Daydream Believers DVD Commentary

480 Getlen, L, "Fame & Fortune: Davy Jones", Bankrate

481 Getlen, L, "Fame & Fortune: Davy Jones", Bankrate

482 Daydream Believers DVD Commentary

483 Daydream Believers DVD, November 2001

484 Daydream Believers DVD Commentary

485 Robbins, C, "Hey Hey It's The Monkees' Davy Jones", *BWW Interviews*, 25 Aug 25, 2011

486 Dakota Radio, Live Radio Show Deadwood, 21 October 2011

487 "Davy Jones: Where are they now, Australia", 2007

488 Cortez, C, "In Memorium - One of the last interviews with The Monkees' Davy Jones", original interview summer 2011

489 Baker, A, "Monkee Mania", 1989

490 James, G, "Interview With Davy Jones Of The Monkees:, www.classicbands.com/DavyJonesInterview.html

491 Daydream Believers DVD Commentary

492 Baker, A, "Monkee Mania", 1989

493 "Davy Jones Talks About Everything", *Flip*, Aug 1967

494 Daydream Believers DVD Commentary

495 Spin Cycle Post, *Daydream Believers DVD*, 14 November 2001

496 Daydream Believers DVD Commentary

497 Hunniford, G, Celebs Up Close with Gloria Hunniford, 1984

498 Daydream Believers DVD Commentary

499 Baker, A, "Monkee Mania", 1989

500 Daydream Believers DVD Commentary

501 Daydream Believers DVD Commentary

502 Baker, A, "Monkee Mania", 1989

503 Dakota Radio, Live Radio Show Deadwood, 21 October 2011

504 "Hey, Hey, We're The Monkees", Harold Bronson, 1996

505 "Hey, Hey, We're The Monkees", Harold Bronson, 1996

506 "Davy Jones Talks About Everything", *Flip*, Aug 1967

507 "Davy Jones Interview: Monkees/Memoir", Reelin' In The Years, 1988

508 "Davy Jones Interview: Monkees/Memoir", Reelin' In The Years, 1988

509 Daydream Believers DVD Commentary

510 "Hey, Hey, We're The Monkees", Harold Bronson, 1996

511 Daydream Believers DVD Commentary

512 *16 Magazine*, July 1968

513 *16 Magazine*, August 1968

514 Daydream Believers DVD Commentary

515 Head Commentary

516 "Davy Jones Interview: Monkees/Memoir", Reelin' In The Years, 1988

517 Daydream Believers DVD Commentary

518 The Monkees - Davy Jones/Biography, YouTube

519 "Davy Jones Interview: Monkees/Memoir", Reelin' In The Years, 1988

520 "Hey, Hey, We're The Monkees", Harold Bronson, 1996

521 Daydream Believers DVD Commentary

522 Baker, A, "Monkee Mania", 1989

523 James, G, "Interview With Davy Jones Of The Monkees:, www.classicbands.com/DavyJonesInterview.html

524 Daydream Believers DVD Commentary

525 British Film Institute, www.youtube.com/watch?v=SsZcs_4Nznc, 1968

526 British Film Institute, www.youtube.com/watch?v=SsZcs_4Nznc, 1968

527 Baker, A, "Monkee Mania", 1989

528 Daydream Believers DVD Commentary

529 Baker, A, "Monkee Mania", 1989

530 "Monkees Davy Jones," Good Morning San Diego, 31 December 2011

531 "Davy Jones: Where are they now, Australia", 2007

532 Fantaskey Kazuba, B,"Monkee in the Middle of Nowhere", The Best of Central PA 2000 magazine, December 2000

533 Harper, S, "The Monkees: Davy Jones In Conversation: Our salute to a pop great." www.clashmusic.com/features/the-monkees-davy-jones-in-conversation

534 *Tiger Beat*, January 1967

535 Real Deal Bob Steal, March 2001

536 Dominic, S, Mesa Tribune, 1997

537 Getlen, L, "Fame & Fortune: Davy Jones", Bankrate

538 Head DVD Commentary

539 Spin Cycle Post, *Daydream Believers DVD*, 14 November 2001

540 "The Littlest Monkee Is Still Going Strong", Chicago Tribune, 28 January 2011

541 Real Deal Bob Steal, March 2001

542 WPNC Magic 95.9 Radio, July 2001

543 The Original 70's Soundtrack, Alan Barnes and Sue Steward, 96.5 WCTG.FM, November 2010

544 Lina Das, Mailonline

545 www.chroniclelive.co.uk/whats-on/music/interview-davy-jones-monkees-1398185

546 WPNC Magic 95.9 Radio, July 2001

547 Roch Parisien's Rocon Communications, October 1990

548 Jones, D, Celebrity Interview Davy Jones, www.celebrityparentsmag.com/parenting/celebrity-interview-the-monkees-davy-jones

549 "Hey, Hey, We're The Monkees", Harold Bronson, 1996

550 WPNC Magic 95.9 Radio, July 2001

551 Harper, S, "The Monkees: Davy Jones In Conversation: Our salute to a pop great." www.clashmusic.com/features/the-monkees-davy-jones-in-conversation

552 www.philmusic.charmingflowers.com.vn/surprising-news-a-cut-interview-with-davy-jones-from-1997-just-surfaced-in-which-he-revealed-that

553 "Davy Jones: "Being a Monkee Has Been My Greatest Success so Far"", Monkee Spectacular Reprint, 1987

554 Jones, D, "Davy Jones Interview: Monkees/Memoir", Reelin' In The Years, 1988

555 Live at BB King Club, New York, Feb 2012

556 "Hey, Hey, We're The Monkees", Harold Bronson, 1996

557 Harris, D, "Retro Rewind, Conversation with Davy Jones", 2008

558 Bailey, Rob, "David vs. Davy", Back Talk, www.silive.com/entertainment/music/2008/09/, Sep 2008

559 https://www.youtube.com/watch?v=UUVu7oec6rg

560 Bailey, Rob, "David vs. Davy", Back Talk, www.silive.com/entertainment/music/2008/09/, Sep 2008

561 Daydream Believers DVD Commentary

562 https://www.youtube.com/watch?v=UUVu7oec6rg

563 Cortez, C, "In Memorium – One of the last interviews with The Monkees' Davy Jones", original interview summer 2011

564 *Tiger Beat Presents Davy Jones,* December 1967

565 Daydream Believers DVD Commentary

566 "Hey, Hey, We're The Monkees", Harold Bronson, 1996

567 Spin Cycle Post, *Daydream Believers DVD*, 14 November 2001

568 Daydream Believers DVD Commentary

569 "Hey, Hey, We're The Monkees", Harold Bronson, 1996

570 "The Monkees - Davy Jones/Biography", YouTube

571 Davy and Sarah Jones on Pebble Mill, March 1997

572 Daydream Believers DVD Commentary

573 Burns, M, Profiles Featuring Davy Jones. 7 Apr 2010

574 Cortez, C, "In Memorium - One of the last interviews with The Monkees' Davy Jones", original interview summer 2011

575 Daydream Believers DVD Commentary

576 Daydream Believers DVD Commentary

577 Daydream Believers DVD Commentary

578 Daydream Believers DVD Commentary

579 Daydream Believers DVD Commentary

580 Baker, A, "Monkee Mania", 1989

581 British Film Institute, www.youtube.com/watch?v=SsZcs_4Nznc, 1968

582 British Film Institute, www.youtube.com/watch?v=SsZcs_4Nznc, 1968

583 British Film Institute, www.youtube.com/watch?v=SsZcs_4Nznc, 1968

584 British Film Institute, www.youtube.com/watch?v=SsZcs_4Nznc, 1968

585 Harris, D, "Retro Rewind, Conversation with Davy Jones", 2008

586 *16 Magazine*, February 1967

587 "Davy Talking on the Transatlantic Phone", Monkees Monthly, April 1968

588 *16 Magazine*, March 1968

589 *16 Magazine*, May 1968

590 Daydream Believers DVD Commentary

591 *Tiger Beat*, April 1967

592 *16 Magazine*, March 1968

593 16 Magazine, July 1968

594 https://www.youtube.com/watch?v=UUVu7oec6rg

595 Fantaskey Kazuba, B,"Monkee in the Middle of Nowhere", The Best of Central PA 2000 magazine, December 2000

596 Fantaskey Kazuba, B,"Monkee in the Middle of Nowhere", The Best of Central PA 2000 magazine, December 2000

597 Fantaskey Kazuba, B,"Monkee in the Middle of Nowhere", The Best of Central PA 2000 magazine, December 2000

598 Real Deal Bob Steal, March 2001

599 Harris, D, "Retro Rewind, Conversation with Davy Jones", 2008

600 "Davy Jones Talks About Everything", *Flip*, Aug 1967

601 Overbea, L, "Monkees: Hard workers with varied opinions"

602 "Davy Jones Talks About Everything", *Flip*, Aug 1967

603 British Film Institute, www.youtube.com/watch?v=SsZcs_4Nznc, 1968

604 "Davy Jones Talks About Everything", *Flip*, Aug 1967

605 British Film Institute, www.youtube.com/watch?v=SsZcs_4Nznc, 1968

606 Harris, D, "Retro Rewind, Conversation with Davy Jones", 2008

607 Harris, D, "Retro Rewind, Conversation with Davy Jones", 2008

608 Newsom, J, "Davy Jones: The Way You Hoped He'd Be", Veem Magazine, October 15, 2011

609 The Original 70's Soundtrack, Alan Barnes and Sue Steward, 96.5 WCTG.FM, November 2010

610 Davy Jones: Horsin' Around; Living in TV Land, 2006

611 Spatz, D, "Curtain Call with Davy Jones", 1994

612 British Film Institute, www.youtube.com/watch?v=SsZcs_4Nznc, 1968

613 Spatz, D, "Curtain Call with Davy Jones", 1994

614 Spin Cycle Post, *Daydream Believers DVD*, 14 November 2001

615 Harris, D, "Retro Rewind, Conversation with Davy Jones", 2008

616 Harris, D, "Retro Rewind, Conversation with Davy Jones", 2008

617 Harper, S, "The Monkees: Davy Jones In Conversation: Our salute to a pop great." www.clashmusic.com/features/the-monkees-davy-jones-in-conversation

618 https://www.youtube.com/watch?v=UUVu7oec6rg

619 Dakota Radio, Live Radio Show Deadwood, 21 October 2011

620 British Film Institute, www.youtube.com/watch?v=SsZcs_4Nznc, 1968

621 Bernstein, A, "Interview with Monkees member Davy Jones on MUSIC: 60s POP ROCK" by A Bernstein, Assignment x, 2 Dec 2011

622 Spin Cycle Post, *Daydream Believers DVD*, 14 November 2001

623 "Davy Remembers His Mother", *Tiger Beat*, May 1968

624 British Film Institute, www.youtube.com/watch?v=SsZcs_4Nznc, 1968

625 "Davy Jones Talks About Everything", *Flip*, Aug 1967

626 Pick, C, www.godreports.com, "Davy Jones of the Monkees: clues to his love for God", March 2012

627 https://www.youtube.com/watch?v=UUVu7oec6rg

628 Live at the Four Queens in Las Vegas, 31 October 31, 1993

629 James, G, "Interview With Davy Jones Of The Monkees:, www.classicbands.com/DavyJonesInterview.html

630 Daydream Believers DVD Commentary

631 Das, L, "What A Cheeky Monkee", May 2011

632 Live at BB King Club, New York, Feb 2012

633 Live at BB King Club, New York, Feb 2012

634 Gross, M. J, *Celebrity Biograph,* "Davy Jones Interview" Youtube, September 2011

635 "Backstage Pass", Blast from the Past, CD ROM game

636 James, G, "Interview With Davy Jones Of The Monkees:, www.classicbands.com/DavyJonesInterview.html

637 The Howard Stern Show, April 1992

638 Live at BB King Club, New York, Feb 2012

639 Fantaskey Kazuba, B,"Monkee in the Middle of Nowhere", The Best of Central PA 2000 magazine, December 2000

640 "Monkees Davy Jones," Good Morning San Diego, 31 December 2011

641 Robbins, C, "Hey Hey It's The Monkees' Davy Jones", *BWW Interviews,* 25 Aug 25, 2011

642 James, G, "Interview With Davy Jones Of The Monkees:, www.classicbands.com/DavyJonesInterview.html

643 Jan Tuckwood, J, "How My First 'Love' from The Monkees Became My Friend", Feb 2012

644 Daydream Believers DVD Commentary

645 "Davy Jones Talks About Everything", *Flip*, Aug 1967

646 Daydream Believers DVD Commentary

647 The Monkees - Davy Jones/Biography, YouTube

648 Daydream Believers DVD, November 2001

649 Daydream Believers DVD, November 2001

650 Johnny J. Blair, Billtown Bus Stop Radio Hour, 7 Dec 2009

651 Daydream Believers DVD Commentary

652 Daydream Believers DVD Commentary

653 "Hey, Hey, We're The Monkees", Harold Bronson, 1996

654 British Film Institute, www.youtube.com/watch?v=SsZcs_4Nznc, 1968

655 British Film Institute, www.youtube.com/watch?v=SsZcs_4Nznc, 1968

656 British Film Institute, www.youtube.com/watch?v=SsZcs_4Nznc, 1968

657 British Film Institute, www.youtube.com/watch?
v=SsZcs_4Nznc, 1968

658 Spin Cycle Post, *Daydream Believers DVD*, 14 November
2001

659 Davy Jones: Horsin' Around; Living in TV Land, 2006

660 Roch Parisien's Rocon Communications, October 1990

661 Harris, W, "Rescued from the Archives: Remembering
Mr. Jones: Farewell to a Monkee," That Thing They Did,
2012

662 The Original 70's Soundtrack, Alan Barnes and Sue
Steward, 96.5 WCTG.FM, November 2010

663 Harris, W, "Rescued from the Archives: Remembering
Mr. Jones: Farewell to a Monkee," That Thing They Did,
2012

664 Getlen, L, "Fame & Fortune: Davy Jones", Bankrate

665 "Davy Talks About Acting", Tiger *Beat*, November 1967

666 Daydream Believers DVD Commentary

667 Newsom, J, "Davy Jones: The Way You Hoped He'd Be",
Veem Magazine, 15 October 2011

668 "The Monkees - Davy Jones/Biography", YouTube

669 *Tiger Beat*, January 1967

670 "Davy Jones Interview: Monkees/Memoir", Reelin' In
The Years, 1988

671 British Film Institute, www.youtube.com/watch?v=SsZcs_4Nznc, 1968

672 Samuals, L, "Davy Jones Faces Viet Nam and Says: 'I Don't Want to Kill Anybody'", Teen Life, August 1967

673 Samuals, L, "Davy Jones Faces Viet Nam and Says: 'I Don't Want to Kill Anybody'", Teen Life, August 1967

674 The Time of Your Life hosted by Noel Edmonds on BBC1, 1984

675 British Film Institute, www.youtube.com/watch?v=SsZcs_4Nznc, 1968

676 "Davy Jones Faces Viet Nam and Says: I Don't Want to Kill Anybody", *Teen Life*, Aug 1967

677 "Davy Jones Faces Viet Nam and Says: I Don't Want to Kill Anybody", *Teen Life*, Aug 1967

678 "Davy Jones Answers the Questions You've Been Asking" Monkee Spectacular, May 1968

679 Davy and Sarah Jones on Pebble Mill, March 1997

680 Cortez, C, "In Memorium - One of the last interviews with The Monkees' Davy Jones", original interview summer 2011

681 Bernstein, A, "Interview with Monkees member Davy Jones on MUSIC: 60s POP ROCK" by A Bernstein, Assignment x, 2 Dec 2011

682 Jones, D, Bernstein, A, "Interview with Monkees member Davy Jones on MUSIC: 60s POP ROCK" by A Bernstein, Assignment x, 2 Dec 2011

683 The Monkees, Davy Jones Last San Diego Interview with Kevin Fulton, Blog This & Presido Sentinel

684 Twitter account

685 Jan Tuckwood, J, "How My First 'Love' from The Monkees Became My Friend", Feb 2012

686 Milling, R, 2005

687 Davy Jones: Horsin' Around; Living in TV Land, 2006

688 Davy Jones Official Webpage